MINERALS
of the
WORLD

This edition published by
CHARTWELL BOOK
A division of BOOK SALES, Inc
114 Northfield Avenue
Edison, New Jersey 08837
© Copyright Sarl 1995
First English language edition, 1997

Translation: Mark Howarth
English language edition: Cathy Muscat

ISBN: 0-7858-0824-8
Color reproduction by SCAN 4, Spain
Printed in Spain

MINERALS

of the

WORLD

◆

Alain Eid
Michel Viard

C O N T E N T S

Gemstones and Precious Metals

❏

Of the 3,500 mineral species in existence, barely one hundred are classed as gemstones – the term used to describe specimens which can be cut and set as jewels.

Beauty and rarity, however, are not a only defining characteristics. In order for a gem-cutter to work a stone, it must be sufficiently hard to withstand his cutting tools and transparent enough for him to exploit the play of light within. Only diamonds, rubies, emeralds and sapphires possess this combination of qualities in sufficient measure to be called "precious stones" and, between the four of them, represent over 95% of the world jewel trade. The remaining gems are known as "semiprecious stones" and are generally much less valuable than precious stones. There are, however, notable exceptions to this rule. Benitoite, for example, owing to its extreme rarity, can exceed the value of a sapphire of the same carat. Certain stones, such as malachite and rhodochrosite, are unsuitable for cutting because of their structure or opacity. They can, nevertheless, be engraved or sculpted to produce fine decorative objects, in which case they are termed "ornamental stones."

Opposite: Native gold on quartz.

Left: The "Ruspoli" sapphire, a crystal weighing 135.8 carats (27.16g/0.96 oz) which belonged to Louis XIV. Class: oxides.

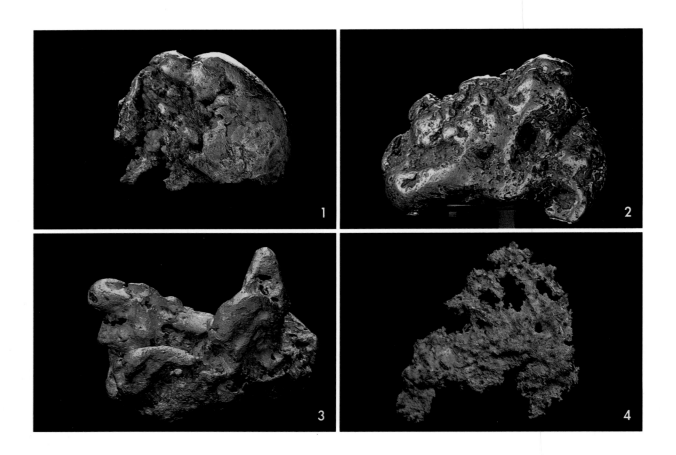

1 and **2** Californian gold nuggets. **3** The "Irma" nugget (8.5kg/3.9 lbs), one of the largest nuggets in a European collection.
4 Californian lamellar gold crystals.

Native gold rarely occurs in perfect geometric crystals. Trapped in rock fissures, its growth is often impeded, creating strange, flattened and plant-like shapes. The characteristic form of alluvial gold is the nugget, found chiefly in riverbeds. They are carried downstream from their source by the current, often over long distances – their smooth and rounded shape the result of rolling over pebbles. They are obtained by washing the sand using a pan, the prospectors' traditional bowl. The largest nugget ever recorded weighed 95kg (209 lbs) and was found in Australia in the last century.

Opposite: Dendritic gold on quartz.

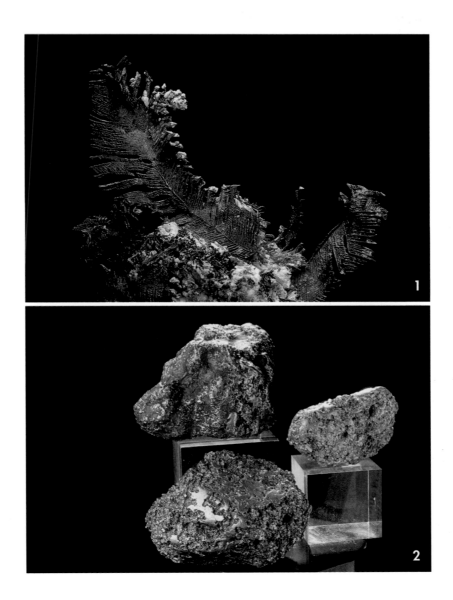

1 Massive silver (dendritic crystals). 2 Platinum.

Platinum is the rarest and most expensive of the precious metals – less than 200 tons are mined each year. It wasn't discovered until the seventeenth century, when the conquistadors went in search of gold in land that is now part of Colombia. As methods for smelting platinum had yet to be discovered, they considered it to be of no value and, owing to its color, gave it the derogatory name of platina, the diminutive of silver. It was not until the eighteenth century, when platinum smelting techniques were developed, that its true value was appreciated. Unlike silver, platinum does not tarnish and possesses a greater density and lustre.
These properties have made it the preferred metal among jewelers for setting precious stones.

Opposite: Native silver with calcite (Mexico).

Silver has always occupied a secondary position to gold because it is much more abundant – 9,500 metric tons (10,500 tons) are mined annually, compared with 1,400 metric tons (1,500 tons) of gold.

Following pages: Faceted sapphires. Class: oxides (Sri Lanka).

11

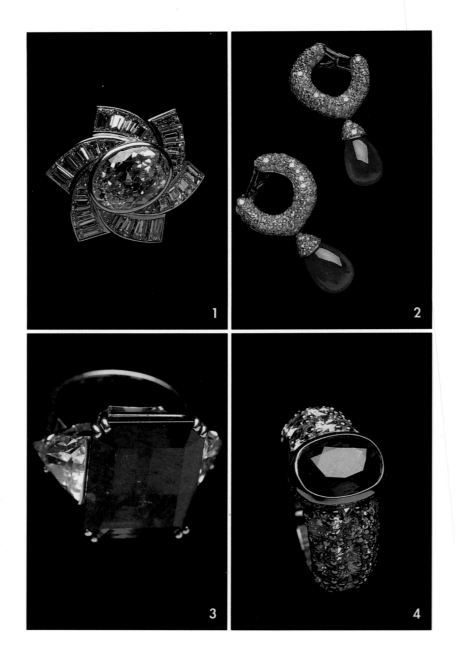

1 Pear cut diamond weighing 4.91 carats (0.982g/.035 oz), set on a ring. **2** Faceted rubies, set as pendants on earrings. **3** Colombian emerald weighing 14.86 carats (2.972g/0.105 oz), emerald cut, set on a ring (approximate value: $560,000). **4** Brilliant cut sapphire from Ceylon weighing 4.09 carats (0.818g/0.029 oz), set on a ring.

Opposite: Emerald cut diamond weighing 6.4 carats (1.28g/0.05 oz), mounted on a ring, with a setting of white and yellow diamonds (approximate value: $200,000).

When extracted from the earth, a raw crystal (even that of a precious stone) lacks any great allure. It requires all the gem-cutter's skill to give it the harmonious shape that will enable a maximum intensity of light to be reflected in it. With its 56 facets, the brilliant cut is the most widely used for gemstones. While traditionally reserved for diamonds, it is suitable for any round stone that, like a diamond, possesses a high refractive index. The graduated square or rectangular cut is known as "emerald," as it intensifies the green of that particular gemstone better than any other cut – though it is by no means exclusive to it. Any shape can be used – pear, heart, rose, baguette, marquise and so on – provided that light enhances the precious crystal.

Following pages: Emerald on calcite encrusted with pyrite. Class: silicates (Colombia).

1 Snakeskin chalcedony. Class: oxides (USA). **2** Chrysoprase chalcedony. Class: oxides (USA). Chalcedony is a fibrous variety of quartz, called carnelian when red, sardonyx when brown, and chrysoprase when tinted green. It was first imported from the Orient via the great Phoenician port of Carthage and its name is thought to derive from the city's former name of Karkhêdôn. According to Pliny the Elder, athletes would wear it on an amulet to ensure victory. **3** Turquoise. Class: phosphates (USA). **4** Aventurine. Class: oxides (Brazil). **5** Blue chalcedony. Class: oxides (South Africa). **6** Olivine (peridot). Class: silicates (USA).

Gem-quality olivine comes principally from Zebirget (or St. John) Island in the Red Sea. The Egyptians were already mining this precious deposit 3,500 years ago and kept it secret for centuries as insurance against plunder – to such an extent that it was ultimately forgotten, with commercial exploitation not recommencing until the start of the twentieth century. The famous eyeglass through which Nero watched the games in the arena was made from olivine.

Opposite: Beryl (heliodor). Class: silicates (Ukraine).

Following pages: Flakes of ruby in zoisite. Class: oxides (Tanzania).

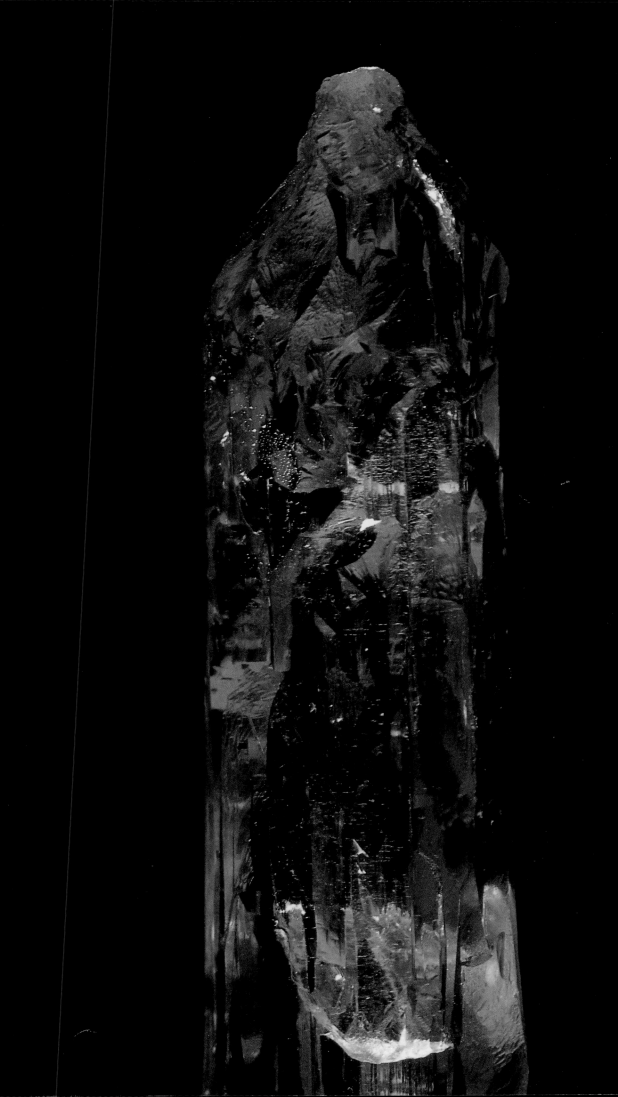

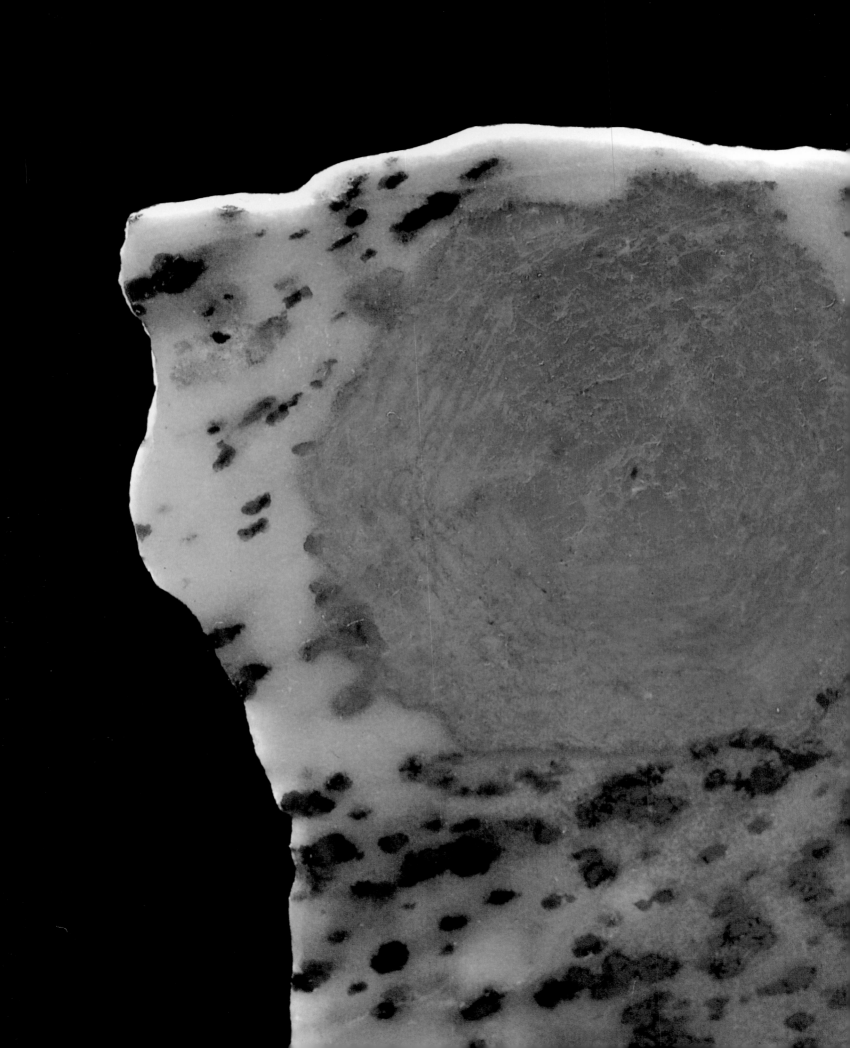

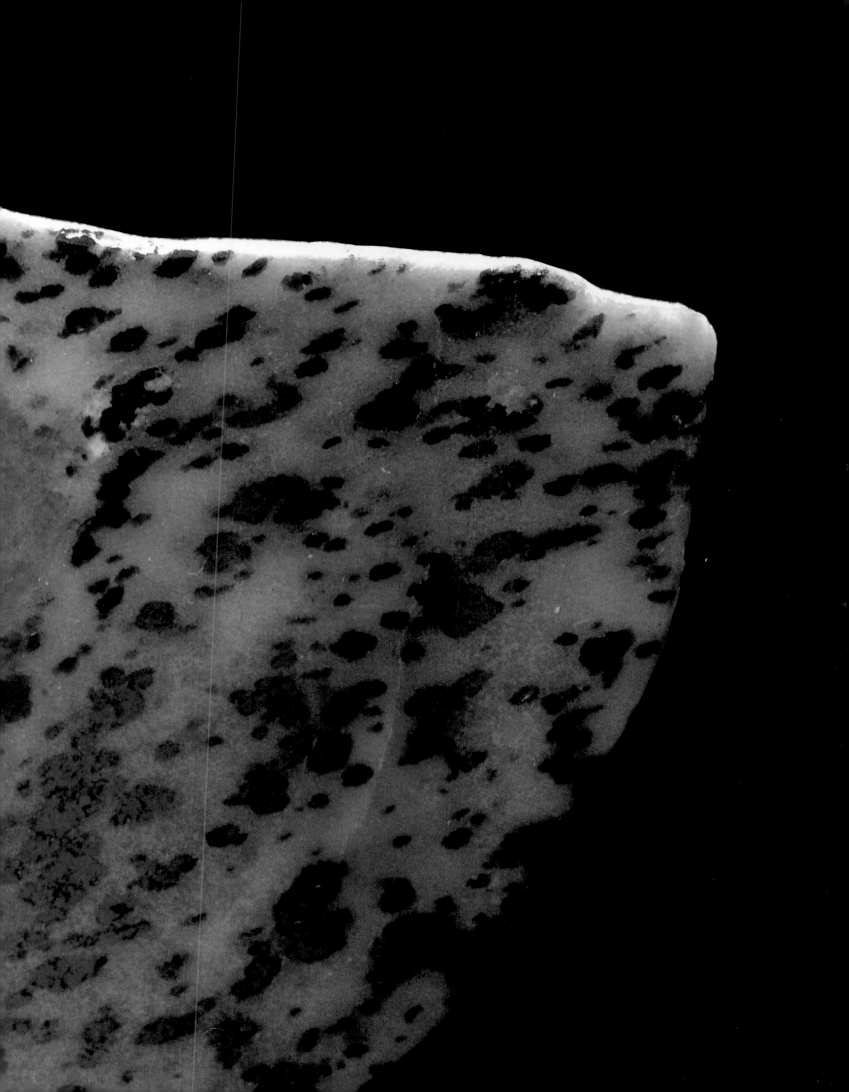

1 Jasper. Class: oxides (France). **2** Adularia (moonstone). Class: silicates (South Africa). **3** Oligoclase (sunstone). Class: silicates (India). **4** Epidote (unakite). Class: silicates (USA). **5** Citrine. Class: oxides (Brazil). Citrine is a yellow form of quartz – mostly amethysts on which the action of heat has produced the yellow coloring. It is sometimes sold as topaz, a practice that is now illegal in some countries. **6** Carnelian. Class: oxides (Brazil). According to tradition, powdered carnelian stops bleeding and removes stains from teeth.

Opposite: Imperial topaz. Class: silicates (Brazil).

Topaz is a deceptive gemstone as it can resemble a diamond in appearance and brilliance. It took some years for experts to realize that the famous 1,680 carat (336g/12 oz) "Braganza" diamond, property of the Portuguese state, was in fact only a topaz. The Ancients called it the "iris stone" because of the way its transparent variety diffracts sunlight, projecting the colors of the spectrum.
Alchemists believed topaz to be capable of curing madness and immunizing against venom. When worn on the left hand, it is said to temper carnal passions.

Following pages: Jewelery set with faceted diamonds (approximate total value: $900,000).

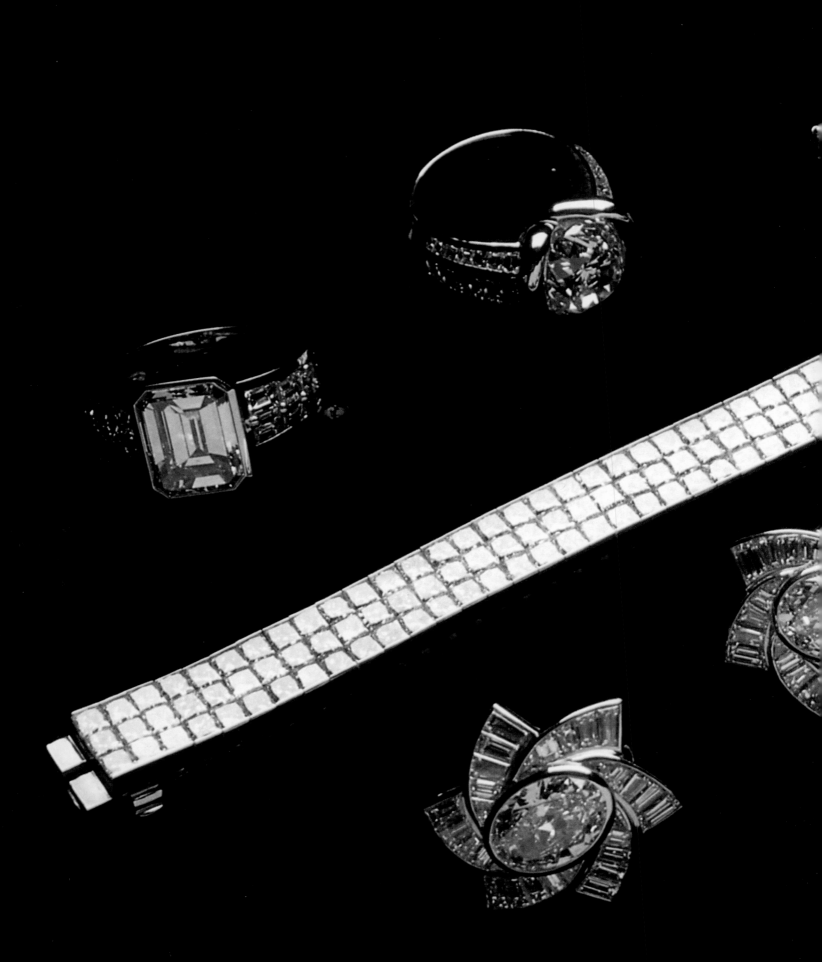

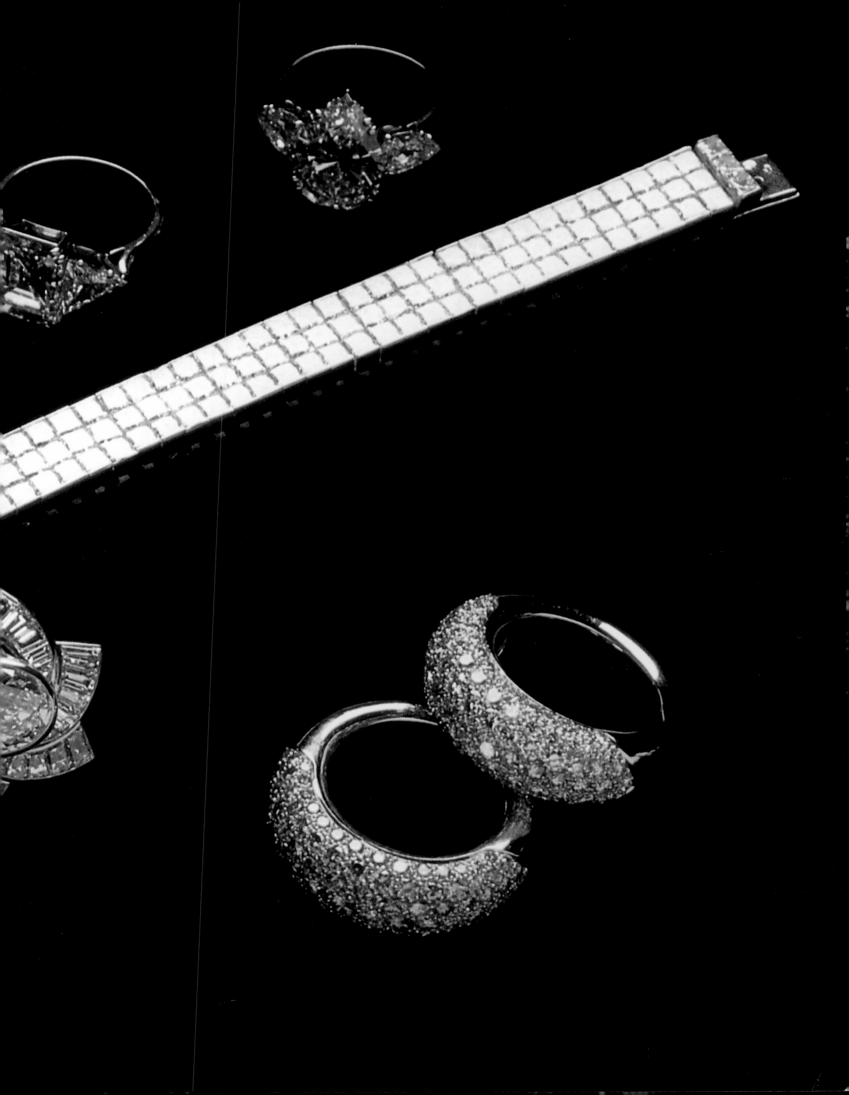

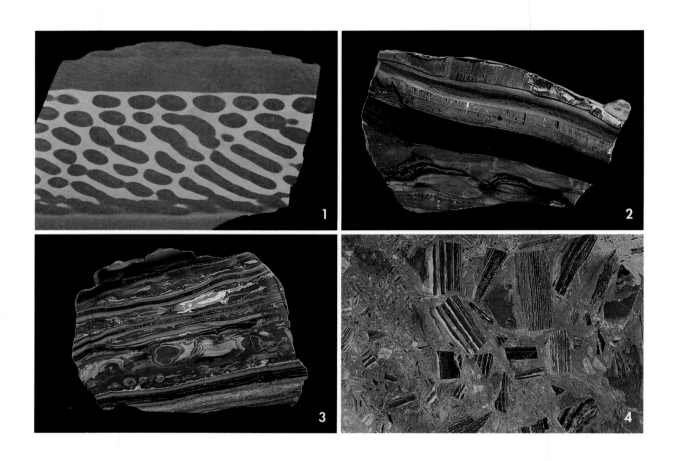

1 Australian zebra stone. **2** and **3** Brazilian jasper. **4** South African brecciate jasper.

Jasper is an opaque, decorative rock composed of 75% quartz. The presence of iron turns it red or green and creates the intricate designs that have led to evocatively named varieties such as "floral jasper," "ribbon jasper" and "agate jasper." In Antiquity, red jasper was recommended to stop bleeding and, when worn on an amulet around the thigh, it was believed to help women during childbirth. In its green form, it became the rain-bringing stone of fertility.

Opposite: Chrysocolla with cuprite. Class: silicates (USA).

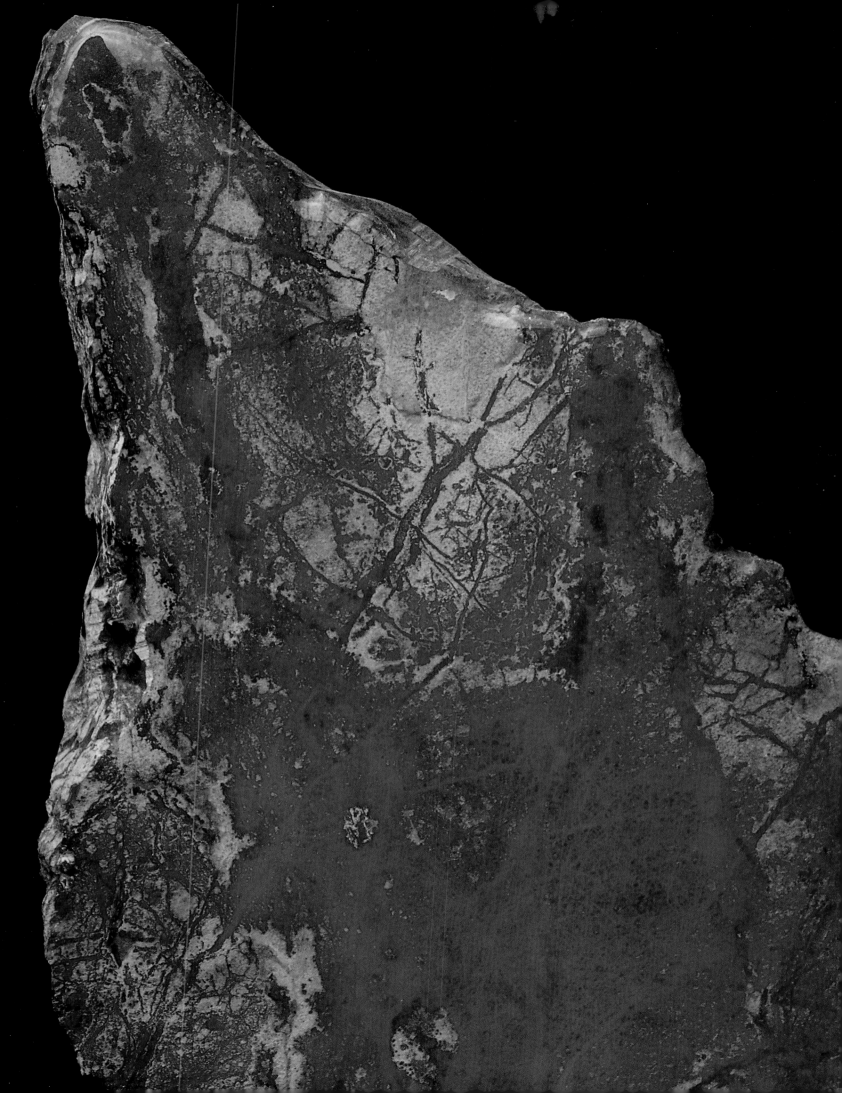

Sapphire Blue

❑

Sapphire is a variety of corundum, an aluminum mineral whose deep blue color results from the presence of iron and titanium. It has long been associated with the realm of the heavens, as though the infinite blue of the skies were reflected in its crystal. The Persians believed that the world was balanced on a sapphire whose brilliance made the sky blue, while a similar reverence led the Hebrews to imagine that God sat on a throne of sapphires. Indeed, it is thought that the word is of Semitic origin and derived from *sappir*, which means "the most beautiful thing." Although yellow, green and violet varieties exist, only blue corundum can be called true sapphire the others are properly qualified as "yellow sapphire" and so on. These are very common and of a much lower value than the blue variety, which is why they are often heated to turn them blue, whereas the red variety is the ruby, occupying a place of its own in the large corundum group. The most beautiful specimens are reputed to come from Kashmir or from Burma, but these have become extremely rare. Today, half of the world's sapphire production is provided by Sri Lanka. The rocks come from the Ratnapura region where they are found by washing and sifting through river gravel, exactly the same method used three thousand years ago. Huge crystals of 100 carats or more are sometimes discovered – the largest ever recorded weighed an incredible 100,000 carats (20kg/44 oz). The sapphire is the only precious stone that naturally occurs in such great masses. While its market price is lower than that of diamond, ruby or emerald, sapphire can nevertheless fetch astronomical sums. A star sapphire, one of the rarest varieties, was sold at auction in New York in 1990 for the not inconsiderable sum of one million dollars.

Opposite: Violet fluorite.
Class: halides (China).

Above: "Cushion-cut" sapphire weighing 16.51 carats (3.302g/0.116 oz). Class: oxides (Sri Lanka).

1 Violet fluorite on calcite. Class: halides (Spain). 2 Violet fluorite on pitchblende and barite. Class: halides (USA). 3 Violet fluorite and barite. Class: halides (Spain). 4 Violet fluorite with galena crystal. Class: halides (England). 5 Violet fluorite with pitchblende. Class: halides (USA). 6 Violet fluorite. Class: halides (Mexico).

Necklaces of fluorite beads have been discovered in the prehistoric caves at La Leisse, in Belgium, indicating that it, along with quartz, was one of the first minerals used by man to make jewelery. The Chinese have an ancient tradition of carving fluorite into little Buddhas, teapots and perfume burners, objects that have been misleadingly sold as green quartz. A great deal of patience is needed to carve this mineral, as fluorite is difficult to work and has a tendency to lose its color when exposed to heat and light. For this reason, it has been little exploited in the western world, apart from by the Romans, who liked to make their libations in fluorite vases (the famous murrha vases).

Opposite: Violet fluorite. Class: halides (Mexico).

Following pages: Blue fluorite on quartz. Class: halides (France).

1 Blue fluorite. Class: halides (England). 2 Blue fluorite with pyrite inclusions. Class: halides (France).
3 Violet fluorite. Class: halides (France). 4 Violet fluorite and barite. Class: halides (Spain).
5 Blue fluorite. Class: halides (France). 6 Blue fluorine. Class: halides (France).

Fluorite is known in industry as fluorspar and is the chief source of the fluoride familiar for its uses in the prevention of tooth decay. Today, many countries regularly add fluoride to their drinking water and table salt, but it is perhaps less well known for its use in producing low temperatures in freezers and air-conditioning systems. The only black mark against its name is the use of gaseous compounds of fluorine in aerosol propellants, which are now known to play an active role in the destruction of the ozone layer.

Opposite: Violet fluorite on quartz. Class: halides (Mexico).

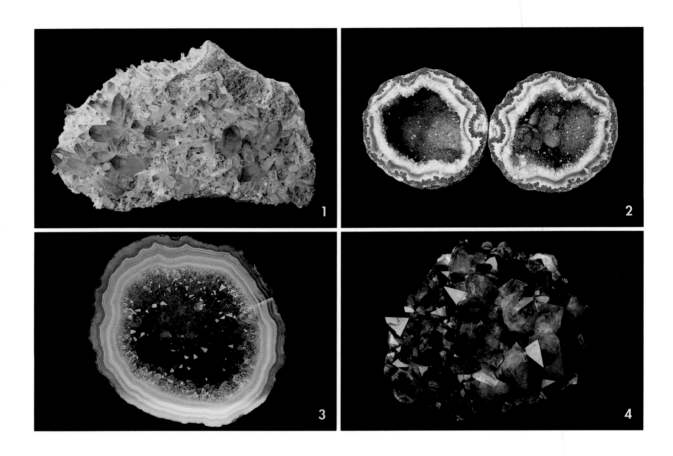

1 "Dog's tooth" amethyst, so called when only the tips of the crystals are colored violet. Class: oxides (Mexico). 2 Amethyst geode with calcite crystals. Class: oxides (Mexico). 3 Amethyst geode with agate margin. Class: oxides (Brazil). 4 Fragment of an amethyst geode. Class: oxides (Brazil).

Amethyst is rock crystal (quartz) that has been colored violet by iron and was traditionally worn to protect against intoxication. This belief has its roots in the legend of Bacchus, the god of wine, who one day fell in love with Amethyst, one of the goddess Diana's nymphs. In order to protect her from Bacchus' amorous advances, Diana transformed her into a rock crystal, making her as pure as she was inaccessible. Bacchus was so heartbroken that he emptied his goblet of wine over the rock, which immediately turned violet. This superstition led to the practice of bishops wearing an amethyst on their finger as a symbol of temperance. For a long time amethyst was hard to find and so was as valuable as other rare precious stones, until the discovery, at the beginning of this century, of huge deposits in Brazil and Uruguay which have yielded crystals weighing several kilograms.

Opposite: Amethyst. Class: oxides (Uruguay).

1 Asteriated sapphire. Class: oxides (France). **2** Celestite geode. The name derives from the celestial blue color of the first specimens discovered, but it is more often white or colorless. It is a source of strontium, a metal similar to calcium, which gives a red color to fireworks and reflective glass for traffic lights. Class: sulphates (Madagascar). **3** Benitoite in white natrolite. Class: silicates (USA). **4** Tetrahedrite. Class: sulphides (France). **5** Chalcedony. Class: oxides (South Africa). **6** Benitoite. Class: silicates (USA).

Discovered in 1906 in San Benito County, California, benitoite is a highly prized stone made all the rarer because the San Benito deposit is the only one in the world. A good, gem-quality specimen weighing over 2 carats (0.4g/0.01 oz) can have a greater value than sapphire, which it resembles.

Opposite: Crocidolite. Class: silicates (Bolivia).

1 Topaz (crystal weighing 2kg/4.4 lbs). Class: silicates (Brazil). 2 Celestite geode. Class: sulphates (Madagascar). 3 Amazonstone microline. Class: silicates (USA). 4 Azurite with cuprite. Class: carbonates (France). 5 Azurite. Class: carbonates (France). 6 Blue beryl. Class: silicates (Pakistan).

Although certain varieties of beryl can produce extraordinary stones, like emerald and aquamarine, the majority have no great value. Because of its transparency, it was used to make magnifying glasses during the Middle Ages, which were known as "beryls."

Opposite: Aquamarine. Class: silicates (Pakistan).

The sea-like color of aquamarine has lent it a lasting association with water – it used to be claimed that mermaids left it on the shore. It is a token of good luck and happiness, and was often carried by those embarking on a long sea voyage.

Following pages: Cyanite (disthene) on quartz. Class: silicates (Brazil).

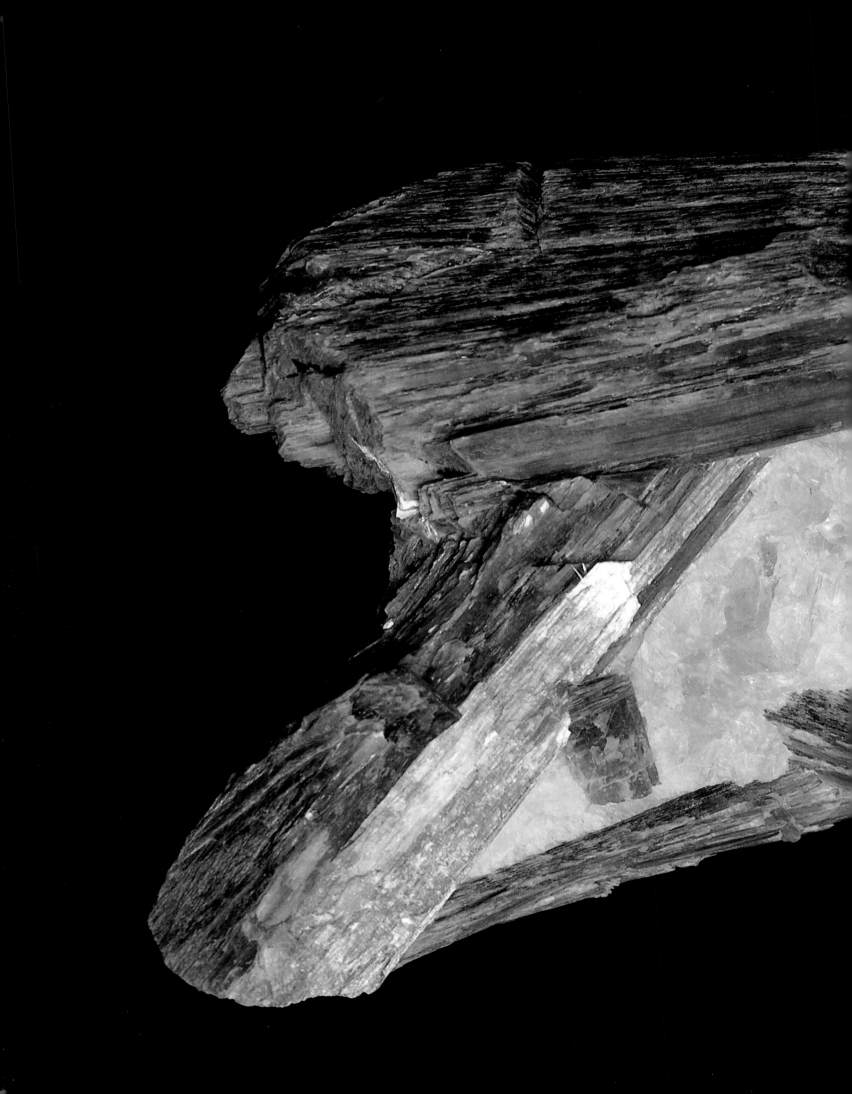

1 Azurite with malachite. Class: carbonates (Morocco). **2** Azurite. Class: carbonates (Namibia). **3** Azurite with malachite. Class: carbonates (Morocco). **4** Stibnite. Class: sulphides (Japan). **5** Azurite with cuprite. Class: carbonates (France). **6** Stibnite. Class: sulphides (Japan).

Stibnite is the chief ore of antimony, a metal which the Greeks called *stibi* (hence its chemical symbol: Sb). It was regarded as a panacea by alchemists, who used antimony's emetic, laxative and diuretic properties in small pellets called "eternity pills." Paracelsus, the Swiss physician and philosopher (1493-1541), prescribed it enthusiastically for the treatment of gout and rheumatism. Legend has it that Basile Valentin, an alchemist and monk from Erfurt, Germany, one day inadvertently gave antimony to some pigs. Having noticed that they became stronger and more vigorous, he decided to repeat the experiment on his fellow monks. However, as it may harbor arsenic, antimony can have unpleasant effects, and many died, hence the origin of the word (from the French *antimoine* – *anti* meaning against and *moine* meaning monk). Stibnite was known long before the discovery of native antimony and was already in use in Egyptian times for eye make-up, as a constituent of the famous Arabic kohl.

Opposite: Azurite geode. Class: carbonates (Namibia).

1 Apatite in quartz. Class: phosphates. 2 Blue indicolite tourmaline in quartz. Class: silicates (Finland). 3 Smithsonite geode. Class: carbonates. 4 Smithsonite. Class: carbonates (Greece). This specimen once belonged to the mineral collection aboard the liner *France*. 5 Linarite on galena. Class: sulphates. 6 Chrysocolla. Class: silicates (Namibia).

Chrysocolla (from the Greek *krusos*, gold, and *kolla*, glue) was long used by goldsmiths as a soldering medium. The famous Eilat stone, the emblematic stone of Israel which was already being worked by the Hebrews when the pharaohs ruled Egypt, is composed partly of it, along with turquoise and malachite. Many "turquoises" discovered in Egyptian tombs are in fact chrysocolla – the two stones are so similar that it remains difficult for the untrained eye to differentiate between them.

Opposite: Turquoise. Class: phosphates (Tibet).

In pre-Columbian America, turquoise was a sacred stone that could be worn only by the Aztec emperor. It was attached to his nose and the ritual piercing of the divine nostril was the equivalent of the coronation of a western king. The most beautiful turquoises come traditionally from the Orient, where they are used as talismans against the "evil eye." According to legend, wearing a turquoise ring protects against fatal falls – should a man fall, the turquoise will shatter in its setting and he will escape injury.

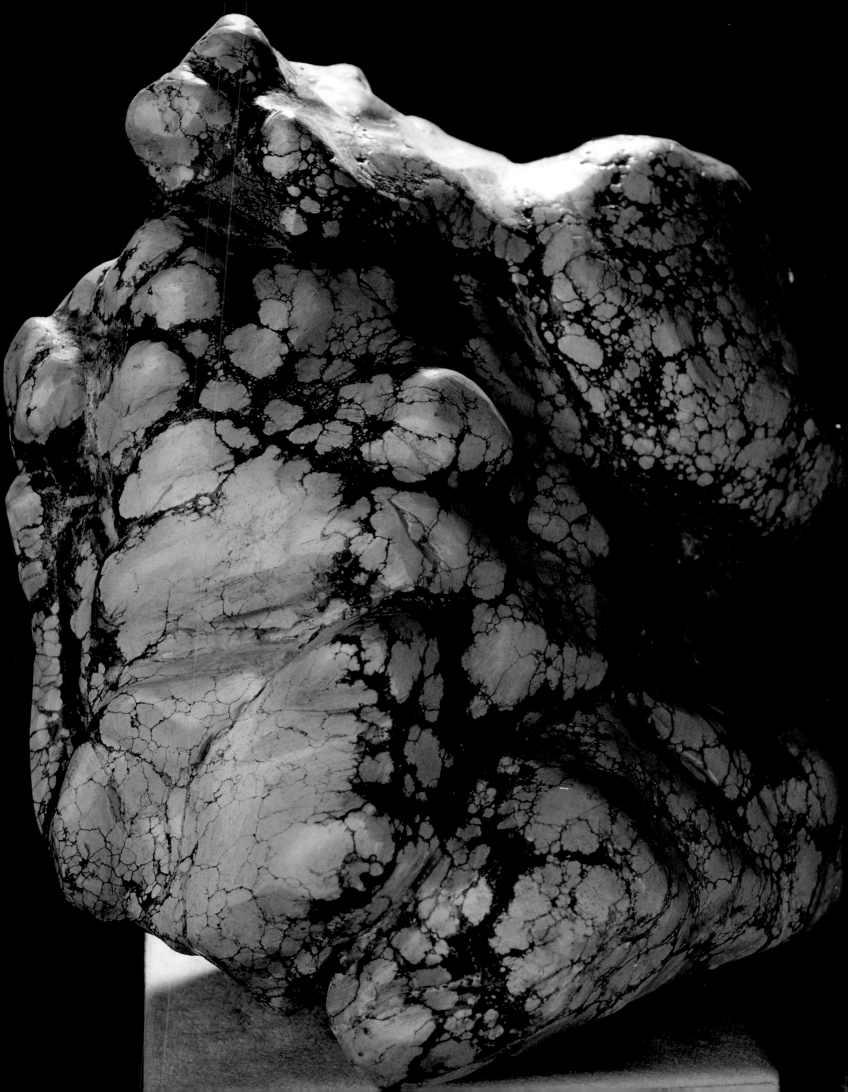

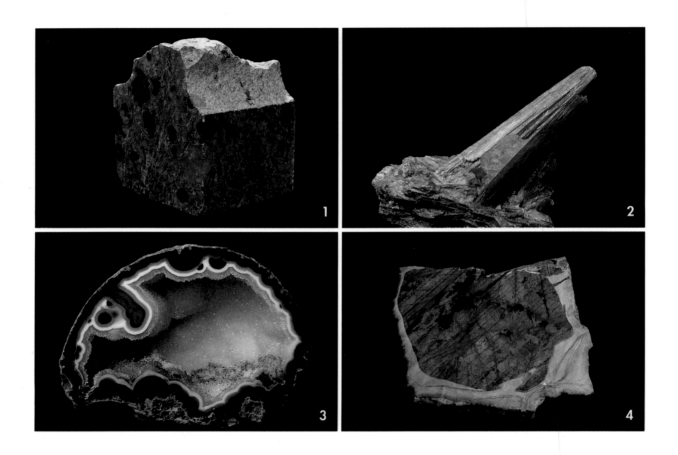

1 Charoite. Class: silicates (Russia). 2 Cyanite (disthene). Class: silicates (Brazil). 3 Diopside geode. Class: silicates (Congo). 4 Labradorite. Class: silicates (Canada).

Opposite: Lapis lazuli (Afghanistan).

Lapis lazuli is a decorative rock composed of lazurite, calcite and pyrite. After six thousand years of mining, the deposit at Sar-e-Sang, Afghanistan, remains the only place in the world where it is extracted. With demand for this precious rock much lower than in the past, barely one metric ton is produced annually. Today, a less costly (but also less beautiful) variety, a type of sodalite, is produced in Chile. The Egyptians were particularly fond of using it to decorate royal tombs and are thought to have invented enamel in their attempts to imitate its beauty. Lapis lazuli was introduced into Europe in the fifth century and was for many years used as a pigment in painting, providing the famous ultramarine. Lazurite, its main constituent, is not to be confused with azurite or lazulite.

Emerald Green

❑

Emerald is the most magnificent of the beryls, and is the most valuable precious stone after diamond and ruby. Its deep green color is due to the presence of chromium, and the crystals often have small inclusions, known as emerald "commas." Although these impurities can contribute to an emerald's beauty, a high percentage of them may alter the stone's transparency, and therefore its value. Since the second millennium BC, emerald has been a highly prized gemstone in the Orient. Egypt became an important emerald producer with the famous mine at Djebel Zabarah, the oldest in the world. The stones mined here adorned the great beauties of Ancient Egypt, from Queen Cleopatra onwards. It was regarded by the upper classes of Antiquity as a prestigious stone and they used it to display their wealth. By the Middle Ages, emeralds had become so rare in Europe that they were reserved principally for the decoration of holy places, such as the reliquary of Saint Genevieve, the patron saint of Paris, set with 175 emeralds. When the conquistadors embarked on the conquest of South America, they were to discover the fabulous treasures of the Incas and the Aztecs, for whom the emerald was a sacred stone. Coffers full of the stones began arriving in Europe. The great Colombian mines at Muzo and Cosquez, already worked by the native Indians, are still in use today and continue to produce the purest emeralds in the world. Emerald is traditionally the stone of truth. There is a superstition that if anybody wearing an emerald ring lies, the stone will immediately shatter. It is true that emeralds are not very shock-resistant and are quite easily damaged. Some have a tendency to become crazed and lose their brilliance over time.

Opposite: Pyromorphite. Class: phosphates (USA).

Right: Faceted emerald weighing 2.31 carats (0.462g/0.016 oz). Class: silicates (Colombia).

1 Pyromorphite. Class: phosphates (France). 2 Pyromorphite on barite. Class: phosphates (France). 3 Atacamite. Class: halides (Chile). 4 Malachite. Class: carbonates (Zaire). 5 Pyromorphite. Class: phosphates (France). 6 Malachite with chalcopyrite and quartz. Class: carbonates.

Malachite has always provided evidence for the presence of rich copper deposits. Owing to its unusual, plant-like appearance, the Greeks named it *malakhé* after a variety of herb. It is one of the oldest cosmetics known to man and was used as long ago as the fourth millennium BC by Egyptian women, who enhanced their eyes with a blend of powdered malachite and red ochre. During the Middle Ages, it was reputed to have medicinal properties and was used, among other things, to treat colic and as a powerful emetic. It is also said that wearing malachite prevents lightning from striking and brings restorative sleep by banishing nocturnal demons.

Opposite: Atacamite. Class: halides (Chile).

Atacamite is a relatively rare copper mineral whose main deposits lie in the Atacama desert, on the west coast of Chile. Before the invention of blotting paper, it was exported to Europe, where it was used in powdered form to dry ink.

1 Duftite with Cobalto-dolomite. Class: arsenates (France). 2 Libethenite. Class: phosphates (Morocco). 3 Garnierite. Class: silicates (New Caledonia). 4 Pyromorphite. Class: phosphates.

Opposite: Tourmaline. Class: silicates (Brazil).

Tourmaline was not discovered until the eighteenth century, on the island of Ceylon, now Sri Lanka. The Sinhalese word *turmalli* means "the stone which attracts ash," because when rubbed with a cloth, tourmaline crystals generate static electricity and attract particles of dust. This phenomenon was quickly seized upon by magicians in Ceylon, who used it to read prophecies from the ashes. The Dutch mariners who brought it to Europe used it rather more prosaically to clean the ash from their pipes. Of the numerous varieties of tourmaline, only elbaite, which can be either green (verdelite), red (rubellite), blue (indicolite) or colorless (achroite), is used in jewelery.

Following pages: Malachite. Class: carbonates (Zaire).

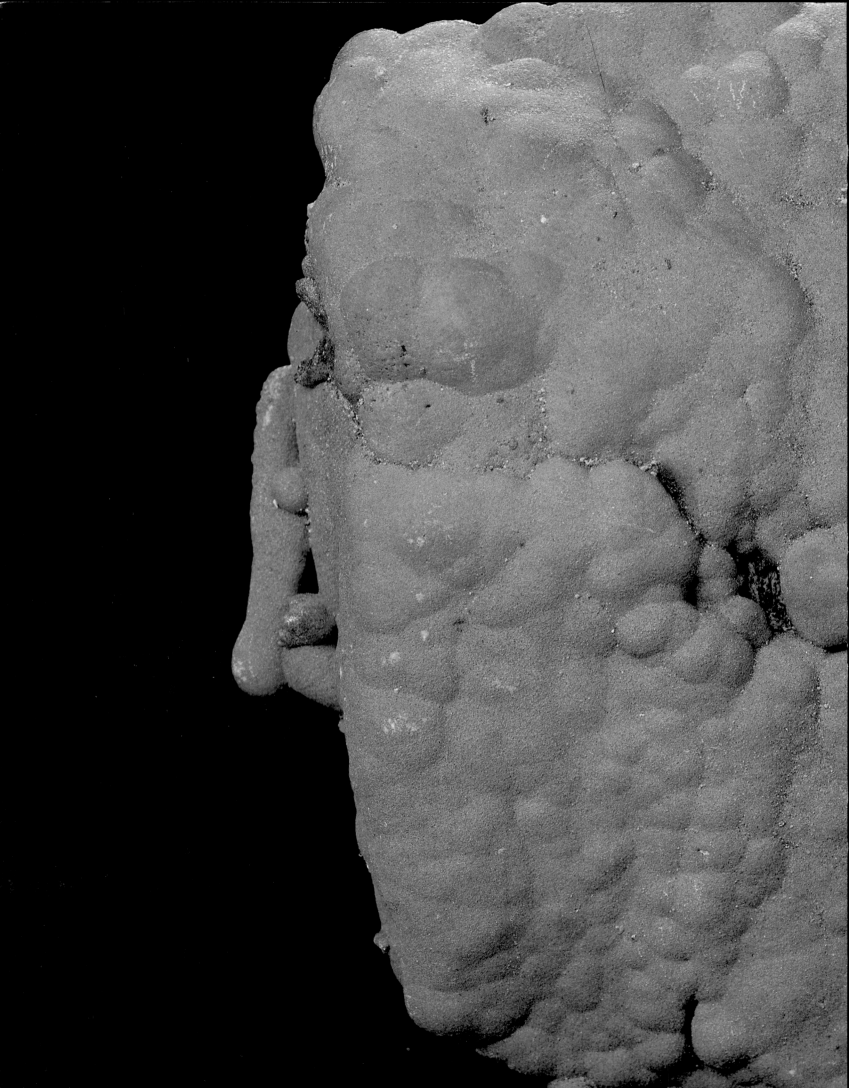

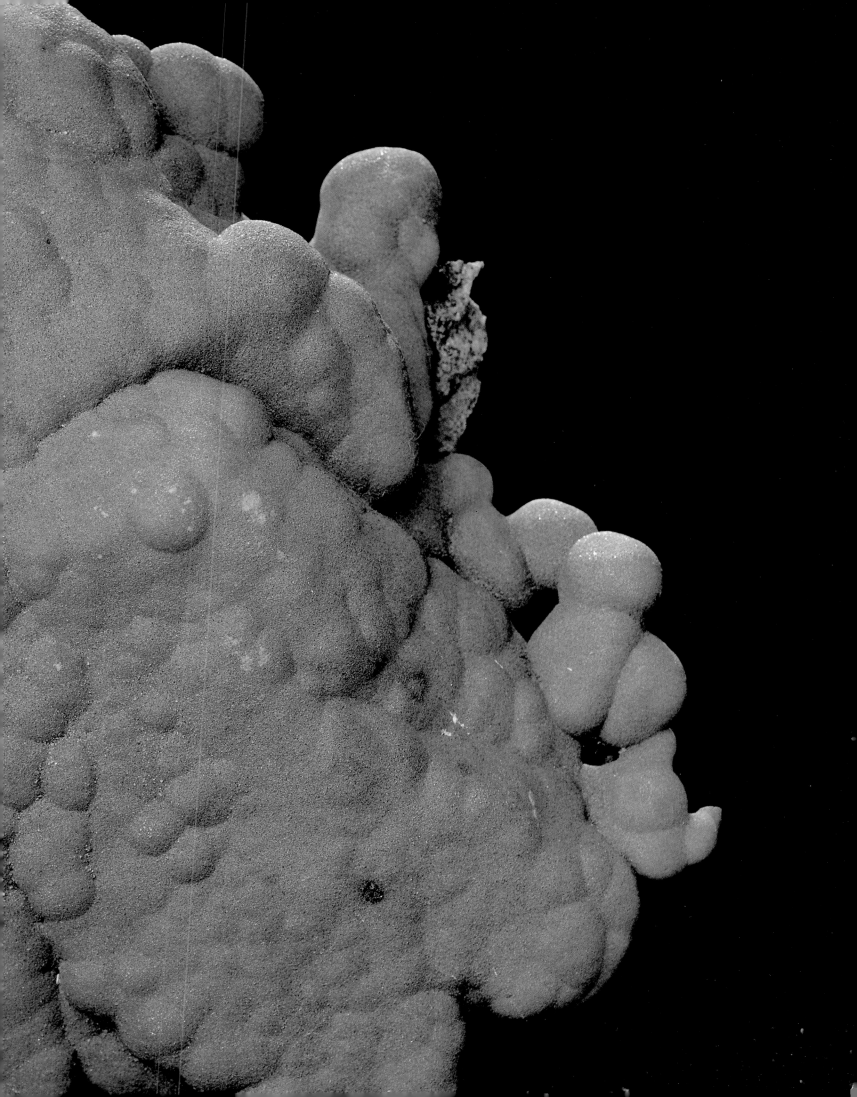

1 Green fluorite. Class: halides (England). **2** Tourmaline (crystal measuring 30cm/11.8 inches). Class: silicates (Brazil). **3** Adamite on limonite. Class: arsenates (USA). **4** Apophyllite. Class: silicates (India). **5** Dioptase. Class: silicates (Congo). The most beautiful dioptases come from the Congo. This rare mineral is among the most sought after by collectors and sometimes occurs in unusual shapes, like this hexagon-shaped specimen. **6** Vivianite. Class: phosphates (Bolivia).

Vivianite may be found as an incrustation in the teeth or bones of fossilized animals – the skull of a mammoth discovered in Mexico had been perfectly preserved owing to the vivianite embedded inside it. These bizarre relics are called "fossil turquoises" because of the resemblance in color and are often sold as turquoise.

Opposite: Amazonstone microcline. Class: silicates (USA).

Amazonstone was discovered in Brazil and owes its name to an Indian legend that tells of warrior women, similar to the Amazons of Greek mythology, who lived in the virgin forest. Once a year, they would enlist the services of men to father their children, paying them with the stone. Amazonstone can occur in enormous crystals, the largest ever found being the 600kg (1,323 lbs) specimen now housed in the National Museum of Natural History, Paris.

1 Topaz. Class: silicates. 2 Prehnite with asbestos and epidote. South African prehnite is known as "Cape emerald," because of its beautiful, translucent and emerald-colored crystals. It is, however, a common mineral, possessing neither the rarity nor value of emerald. Class: silicates. 3 Malachite. Class: carbonates (Morocco). 4 Duftite with calcite. Class: arsenates (Namibia). 5 Moroxite apatite in quartz. Class: phosphates (France). 6 Apatite. Class: phosphates (Portugal).

Apatite is rich in phosphorous and is contained in many different rocks, benefitting the natural world as the soil's chief natural fertilizing agent. Each year, millions of tons of apatite are used as agricultural fertilizer. Phosphorous in our diet helps in the formation of bones and teeth. Apatite often occurs in elongated crystals, resembling tourmaline, or else in crystals similar to beryl or olivine; hence its name, taken from the Greek *apate* meaning "deceit."

Opposite: Beryl. Class: silicates (Brazil).

1 Actinolite. Class: silicates (USA). 2 Wavellite. Class: phosphates (USA). 3 Olivine. Class: silicates (France). Olivine can be found in solidified volcanic lava, as well as in meteorites, but only the variety mined on Zebirget Island, in the Red Sea, is used as a gemstone. The other varieties, however, have great economic value, as they are used to extract magnesium. 4 Minyulite. Class: phosphates (France). 5 Actinolite. Class: silicates (Austria). 6 Muscovite mica, fuchsite variety. Class: silicates (Madagascar).

Of all the different varieties of mica, muscovite is the most common, deriving its name from the region around Moscow where it was produced. Thin, transparent sheets of it were once used for windows in place of glass, and it is still used in some high-temperature industrial furnaces, as it is much more heat resistant than glass. In its powdered form, muscovite is also used in the manufacture of artificial snow for Christmas trees.

Opposite: Minyulite. Class: phosphates (France).

Following pages: Pyromorphite on quartz. Class: phosphates (France).

1 and **4** Green fluorite. Class: halides (England). **2** Pyromorphite. Class: phosphates (France). **3** Aurichalcite. Class: carbonates (Mexico).

Aurichalcite occurs on rock in small, feather-like clusters. While its purpose may seem purely decorative, it is nonetheless an important source of copper and zinc.

Opposite: Amazonstone microcline. Class: silicates (Brazil).

1 Anhydrite. Class: sulphates (Brazil). **2** Watermelon tourmaline. Class: silicates (Brazil). Tourmaline can sometimes occur in bicolor crystals, as here with the watermelon type, where the green crystal is tinged red at the centre. **3** Dioptase with calcite. Class: silicates (Namibia). **4** Tourmaline, variety "verdelite," on quartz. Class: silicates (Brazil).

Opposite: Polished mamillated malachite. Class: carbonates (Zaire).

Following pages: Epidote (pistacite). Class: silicates.

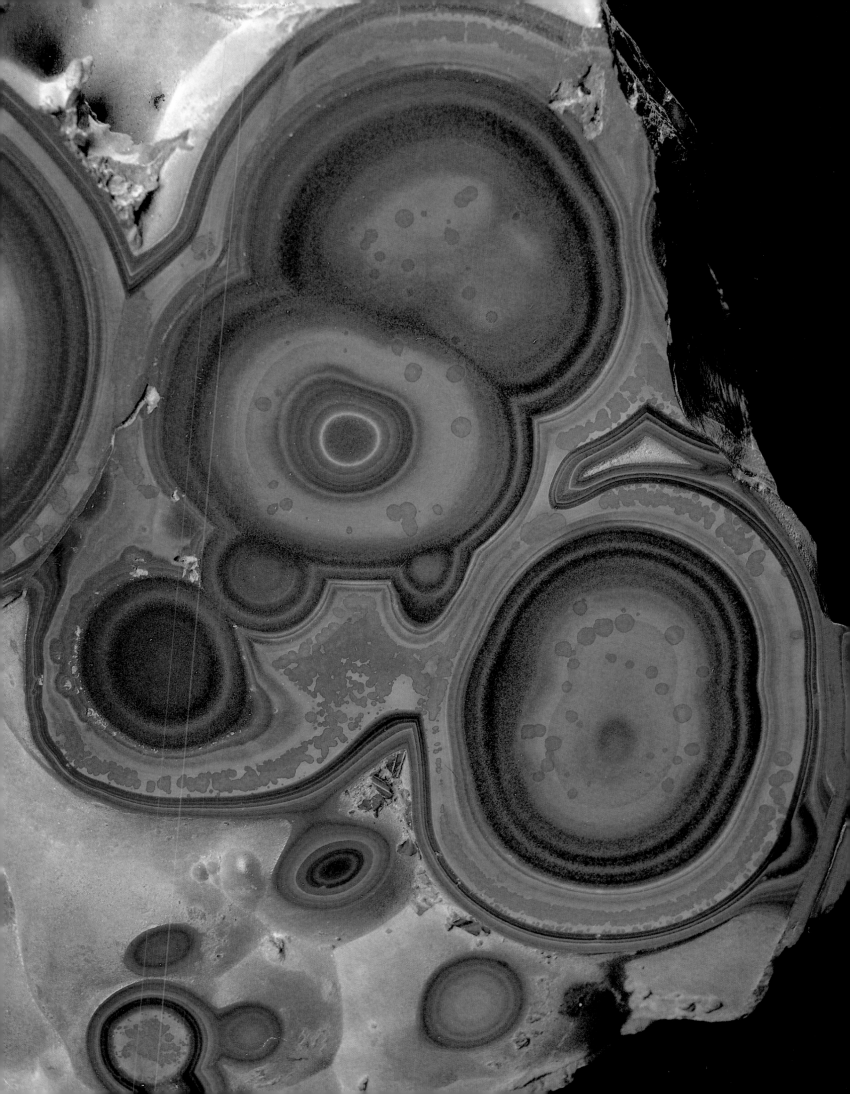

Golden Yellow

❑

Gold has been an object of veneration since pre-historical times. This lustrous metal that burned like the sun was quickly recognized as a precious natural resource and fashioned into jewelery from very early on. It was, in fact, one of the first metals man learned to work. It is so malleable that it can be hammered into paper-thin sheets. By the same token, one gram of gold can be stretched to a length of one kilometer (5/8 mile) without breaking. The total mass of gold extracted to date is estimated at 80,000 metric tons (88,200 tons) and, as the metal is so stable, the majority is still in circulation today. Because it was both durable and rare, gold was quickly established as a means of exchange. The minting of the first gold coins is attributed to Croesus, king of Lydia in the sixth century BC. His name has been synonymous with wealth ever since gold was extracted from the equally legendary river Pactolus in Asia Minor, now known as the Sarabat. Gold deposits were never very common in Europe, and during the Middle Ages the shortage was such that it sustained the alchemists' dream of transforming base metals into gold. It was perhaps their failure to do so that later spurred the conquistadors to cross the Atlantic and seize the gold of the Incas. It could be said that the real "Golden Age" was the nineteenth century, which saw the discovery of rich deposits in California (prompting the great 1848 gold-rush), Australia, South Africa and Alaska.

Opposite: Mica and quartz. Class: silicates.

Above: Californian gold nugget (0.5kg/1.1 lbs).

1 Barite. Class: sulphates (Sardinia). **2** Calcite on pitchblende. Class: carbonates (USA). **3** Bladed gypsum. Class: sulphates. **4** Quartz. Class: oxides (Brazil). **5** Calcite on fluorite and pitchblende. Class: carbonates. **6** Scheelite. Class: tungstates (Korea).

Scheelite is the chief ore of tungsten (or wolfram), a dense metal used in special steel alloys and in the manufacture of the filaments in electric lamps. Its transparent crystals, a delicate shade of amber, are sometimes used as gemstones.

Opposite: Calcite. Class: carbonates (Spain).

Calcite is a very common mineral and the main constituent of limestone and marble. Its name, from the Latin *calcis* or the Greek *khalx*, means lime, which has been extracted since Antiquity by the calcination of limestone rocks. When mixed with water and sand, lime produces building mortar, while cement is made from argillaceous (clayey) limestone.

1 Calcite. Class: carbonates (Mexico). 2 Dolomite with quartz, pitchblende and calcite. Class: carbonates (Yugoslavia). 3 Stilbite. Class: silicates (Australia). 4 Fluorite. Class: halides (France). 5 Fluorite with calcite and pyrite. Class: halides (Spain). 6 Celestite on sulphur. Class: sulphides.

Opposite: Fluorite and calcite. Class: halides (Spain).

Following pages: Sulphur. Class: elements (Italy).

Sulphur occurs in abundance in the earth's crust and is the fundamental element in the sulphate and sulphide groups, to which it has given its name. It melts easily when burned, giving off fumes containing suffocating sulphur dioxide. In Ancient times, homes and public places were regularly fumigated with sulphur as a disinfectant to prevent the spread of disease. Its links with the devil were underlined in the Bible, with the vision of the prophet Ezekiel, who described Satan as "imprisoned in a lake of burning sulphur." This association is due to the fact that native sulphur is most commonly found on the slopes of volcanoes, places connected to satanic power. Sulphur is still used today as a disinfectant and insecticide, as well as in the manufacture of fertilizer.

1 Wulfenite. Class: molybdates (Mexico). 2 Axinite. Class: silicates (France). 3 Barite. Class: sulphates (France). 4 Endlichite. Class: vanadates (Mexico). 5 Campylite. Class: arsenates (England). 6 Brazilianite. Class: phosphates (Brazil).

Brazilianite remained undiscovered until 1945, when two farmers from Minas Gerais state, Brazil, one day dug a large quantity of this unusual, transparent and beautiful yellow stone from their land. They initially identified it as chrysoberyl, a gemstone of great value, and celebrated their windfall. When they came to cut it, they noticed that it showed little resistance to gem cutting tools, owing to its low hardness. Subsequent investigation revealed that it was not a chrysoberyl, but a new mineral, which was named brazilianite after its country of origin. Since then, other deposits have been discovered in Brazil, sometimes yielding crystals over 20cm (8 inches) long. These discoveries have, however, confirmed the results of the early tests: it has beauty, but insufficient hardness to join the elite rank of gemstones. It nevertheless remains a mineral that is highly sought after by collectors, due to its great rarity.

Opposite: Idocrase (vesuvianite) on quartzite. Class: silicates (France).

1 Siderite on calcite. Class: carbonates (Brazil). **2** Columnar prisms of calcite. Class: carbonates (USA). **3** Calcite. Class: carbonates (USA). **4** Smoky quartz. Class: oxides (France). **5** Barite. Class: sulphates (France). **6** Barite and pyrite on a base of iron ore. Class: sulphates (France).

When quartz is turned brown by the presence of a naturally radioactive material, it is known as smoky quartz, huge crystals of which occur in the Swiss Alps. It was here, in 1946, 2,000 meters (650 feet) up the Furka Pass, that a mountaineer discovered a unique lump of this quartz weighing 180kg (397 lbs). He kept his great find a secret and spent weeks bringing it down icy slopes through snow and in bitter cold. Sadly, he never recovered from his superhuman efforts and died a short time afterwards, but his huge piece of smoky quartz can still be seen today at the small village museum in Göschenen.

Opposite: Cleavelandite albite with mica. Class: silicates (Brazil).

1 Sulphur in gypsum. Class: elements (Italy). **2** Diopside. Class: silicates (Madagascar). **3** Aragonite. Class: carbonates (France). **4** Heulandite with stilbite (block weighing 20kg/44 lbs). Class: silicates (India). **5** Flint with chalcedony and quartz. **6** Orthoclase. Class: silicates (Brazil).

Opposite: Flint kidney.

Flint has played a pivotal role in human history, marking the start of civilization over two million years ago. Evidence of this was provided by the discovery of "Olduvai Man" (*Homo habilis*) in Tanzania, in 1953. The unearthed tomb of our ancestor contained numerous items made from flint. Among the tools found, razors, knives, axes and scrapers were clearly recognizable. Flint was also instrumental in the precious discovery of fire, made during the same period. The resulting civilization is aptly called the Stone Age, an era that was to last almost two million years, until the development of metal working. The industrial use of flint did not, however, disappear with the passing of the Stone Age; at the beginning of the last century, it was still used as gunflint and in cigarette lighters.

Following pages: Fluorite with quartz. Class: halides (Brazil).

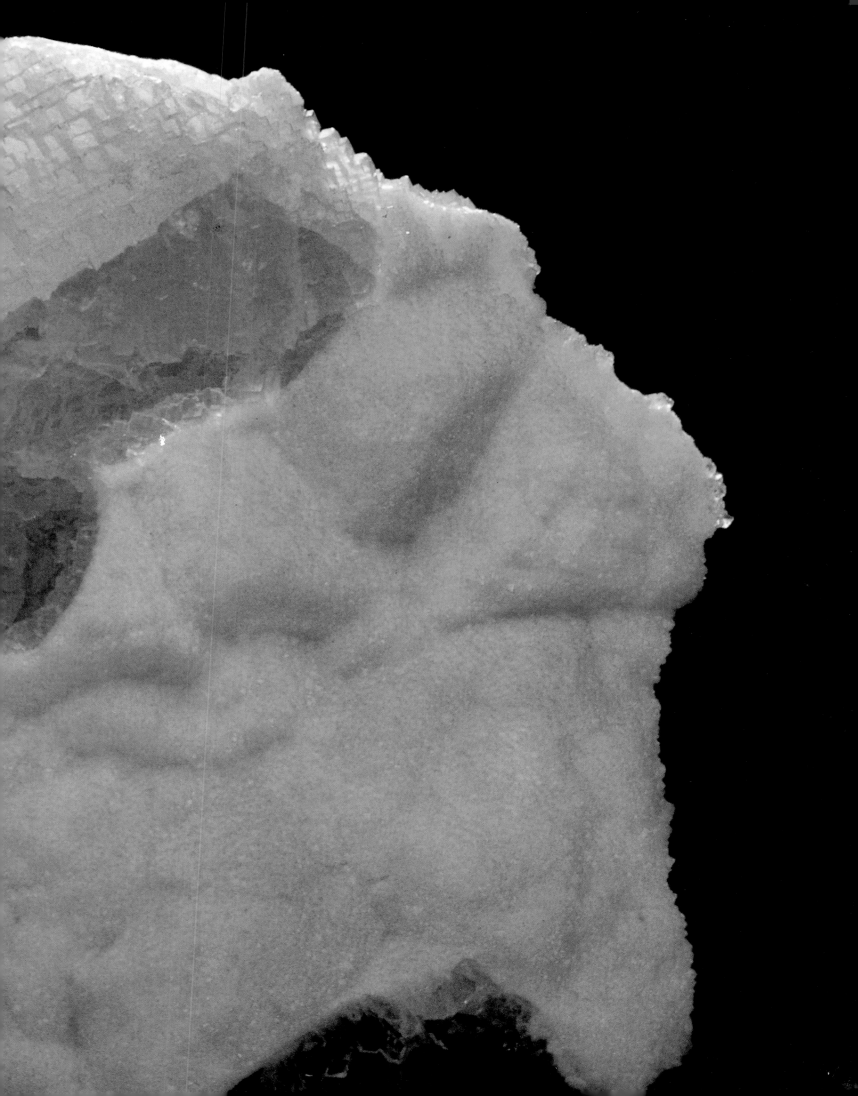

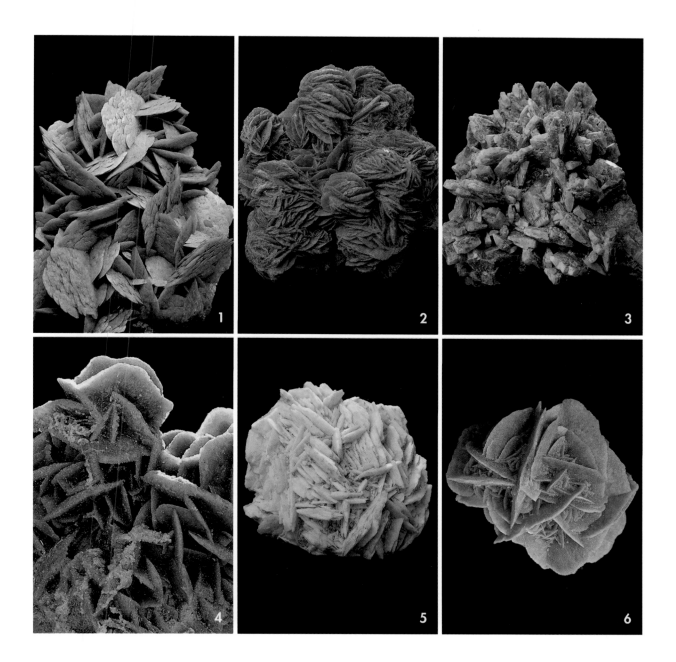

1 Lenticular siderite. Class: carbonates. **2** "Desert rose" gypsum. Class: sulphates (France). **3** Barite. Class: sulphates (France). **4** "Desert rose" gypsum. Class: sulphates (Sahara). **5** Barite "rose." Class: sulphates (France). **6** "Desert rose" gypsum. Class: sulphates (Sahara).

Travelers crossing the Sahara are quite likely to come across what looks like an unusual flower with delicately edged petals, but is, in fact, gypsum whose growth has been altered by the presence of grains of sand in its crystals. Some varieties of barite also occur in this rose-like shape, which is highly valued by collectors.

Opposite: Cerussite. Class: carbonates (Namibia).

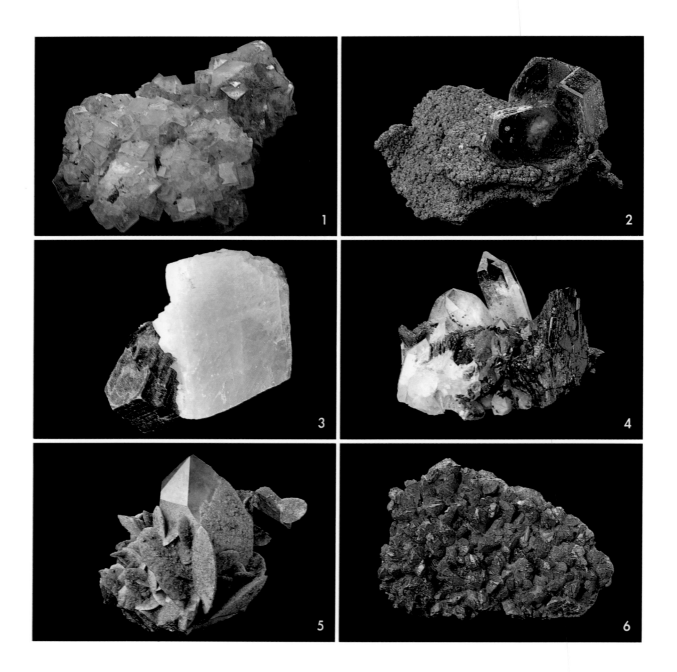

1 Fluorite. Class: halides (France). 2 Apatite. Class: phosphates (Portugal). 3 Mica, phlogopite variety, on calcite. Class: silicates (Madagascar). 4 Arsenopyrite (mispickel) with wolframite and quartz. Class: sulphides (Portugal). Even when only slightly fractured, arsenopyrite gives off the characteristic garlicky smell of arsenic, of which it is the chief source. Its value is all the higher as it often contains gold in sufficient quantities to justify large-scale mining. 5 Siderite with quartz and wolframite. Class: carbonates. 6 Orpiment. Class: sulphides (Peru).

For a long time, orpiment was mistaken for realgar, another important ore of arsenic. They often occur in close proximity around hot water springs. Orpiment has been used for centuries in the Orient for ritual depilation. It also yields a yellow pigment that is much sought after by painters, hence its name, from the Latin *auri* and *pigmentum*, meaning "gold pigment."

Opposite: Barite on pyrite. Class: sulphates (France).

Following pages: Pyrite nodule. Class: sulphides (France).

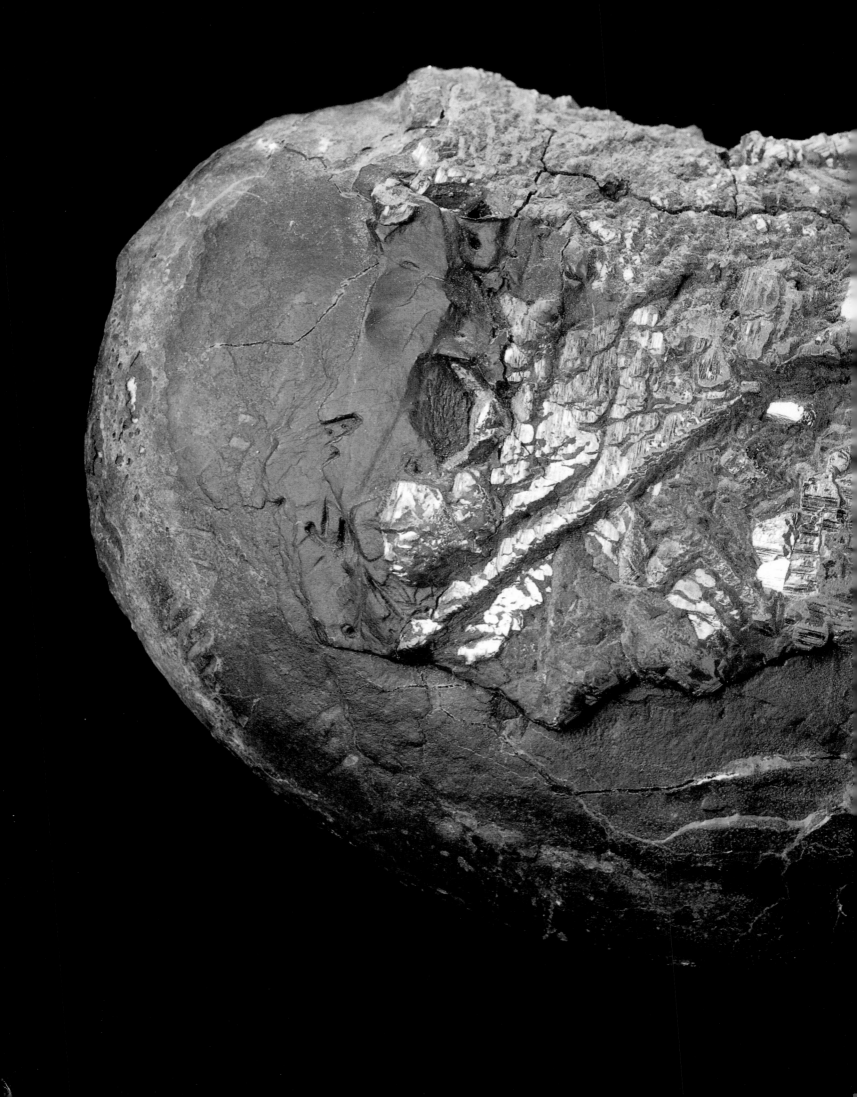

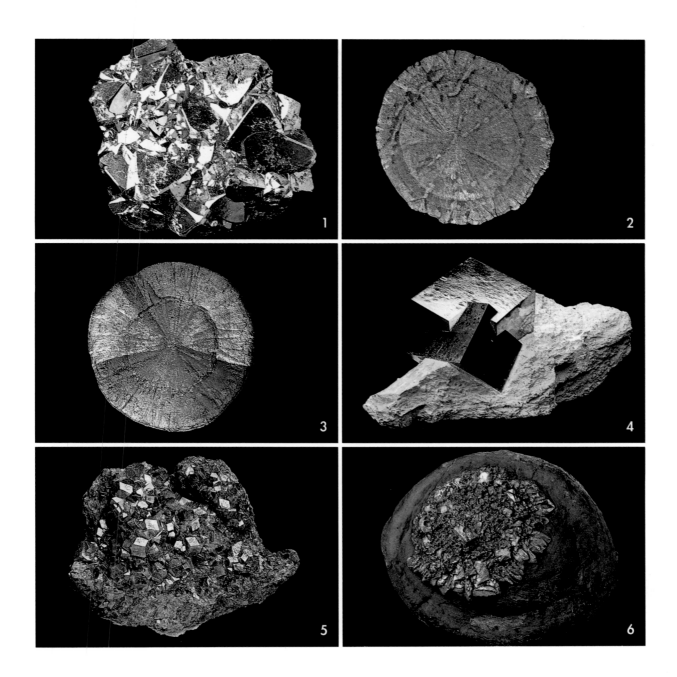

1 Octahedral pyrite. Class: sulphides (Peru). 2 Marcasite "dollar." Class: sulphides (USA). 3 Marcasite "dollar." Class: sulphides (USA). 4 Pyrite. Class: sulphides (Italy). 5 Garnet, andradite variety. Class: silicates (USA). 6 Marcasite. Class: sulphides (France).

Opposite: Pyrite with grains of calcite. Class: sulphides (Italy).

Many prospectors have been duped by pyrite, whose lustre is tantalizingly similar to that of gold. However, this is the only thing that the two have in common – pyrite has one of the lowest market values of any mineral and is therefore sometimes called "fool's gold." Striking pyrite produces sparks strong enough to ignite tinder, and it was in this way that early man mastered fire: striking pyrite with flint. Roman legionnaires were still using the technique centuries later, lighting their fires by striking pyrite with nails. Medicinal properties have long been attributed to pyrite, including its use in powdered form to treat boils and scrofula – a common practice which lasted well into the eighteenth century. As intricately decorated pyrite mirrors were discovered in the pre-Columbian tombs of Peru, it is sometimes called "Incas' mirror."

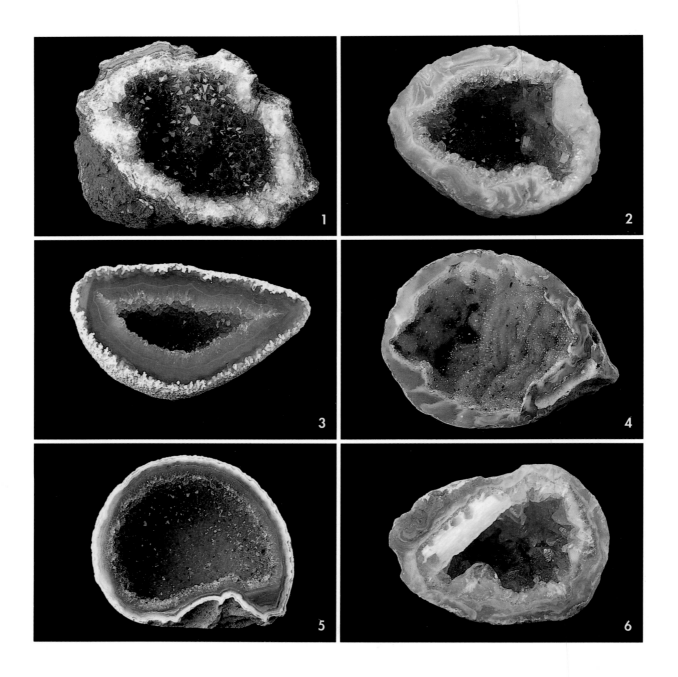

1 to **5** Amethyst geodes. Class: oxides (Mexico). **6** Smoky quartz geode (20kg/44 lbs). Class: oxides (Brazil).

Some minerals, such as various types of quartz, form the lining of geodes, strange rock cavities created initially by gas bubbles trapped in solidifying magma. As a result of a series of chemical reactions, minerals are formed in isolation inside them, usually producing large crystals.

Opposite: Amygdule lined with barite crystals. Class: sulphates (France).

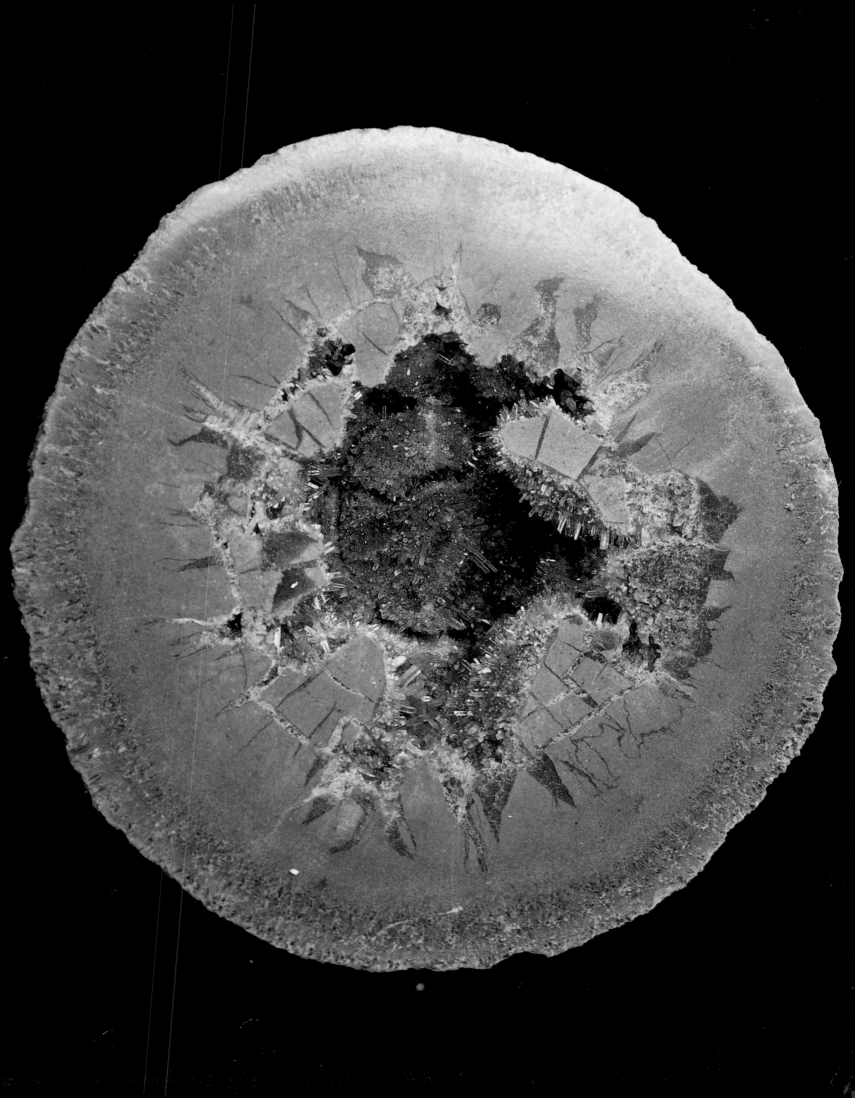

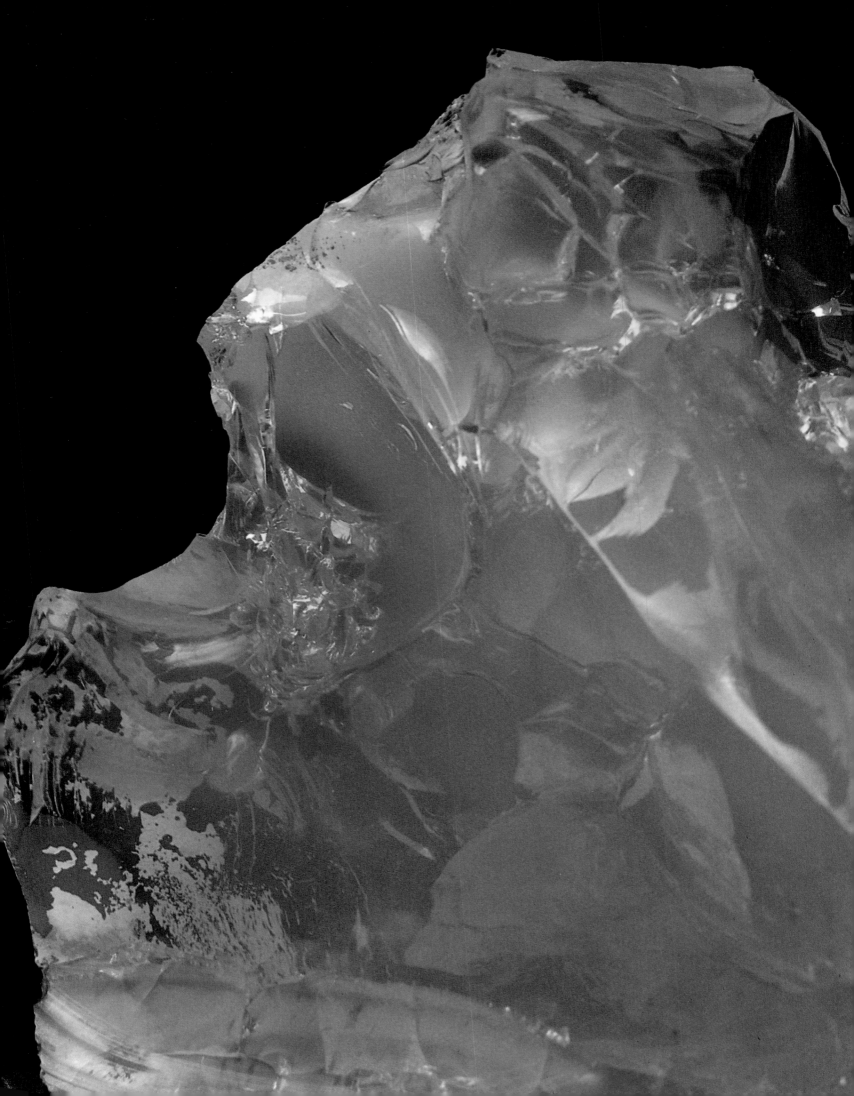

1 Autunite. Class: phosphates (France). **2** Pyromorphite with wulfenite. Class: phosphates (France). **3** Sulphur. Class: elements (Italy). **4** Siderite. Class: carbonates (France). **5** Pyromorphite. Class: phosphates (USA). **6** Pyromorphite on barite. Class: phosphates (USA).

Opposite: Opal. Class: oxides (USA).

According to a recent tradition, dating probably from the last century, opal brings bad luck – a surprising reputation, considering that it had previously been regarded as a "stone of virtue" that protected against misfortune and evil curses. As a result of this unfortunate superstition, opal was banned from the court of Napoleon III. Queen Victoria, on the other hand, took great pride in collecting it, giving it to members of her family as a good luck charm.

1 Aragonite. Class: carbonates (Spain). **2** Calcite. Class: carbonates (England). **3** Barite. Class: sulphates (France).
4 Stibiconite. Class: silicates (Romania). **5** Volcanic bomb from the Massif Central, France.
6 Muscovite mica (block weighing 220kg/485 oz). Class: silicates (Brazil).

Opposite: Barite. Class: sulphates (France).

Unlike gypsum, which it resembles, barite is a mineral of high density, which makes it useful for many industrial applications.
It acts as a good thickening agent for the mud pumped into oil wells to prevent blow-outs.
Millions of tons of barite are used for this purpose each year.

Ruby Red

❑

Ruby is the most prized stone of the richly endowed corundum group. Twenty times rarer than the blue variety, sapphire, its value is markedly higher and only just exceeded by one other precious stone, diamond. A good specimen weighing 10 carats (2g/0.07 oz) can cost over two hundred thousand dollars. The presence of chromium in its chemical composition gives ruby the characteristic color at the root of its name – from the Latin *rubeus,* meaning red. The stones known as pigeon's blood rubies, with their remarkably deep red color, are the most sought after and can command a higher price than diamonds of the same carat. Their beauty is sometimes enhanced by the presence of impurities, called ruby "silks." Thus, small inclusions of rutile can cause the phenomenon of asterism, which creates the appearance of a star moving across the surface of the crystal. Like sapphire, ruby is dichroic and displays two shades of red depending on the direction of light: one dark and intense, the other appreciably lighter.

It was probably this unusual quality that led to the use of rubies in Antiquity for divination. It was considered unlucky if the crystal appeared predominantly dark, whereas a lighter crystal was regarded as a good omen. The most prized rubies traditionally come from Mogok in Burma, where they have been mined for fifteen centuries, providing the finest pigeon's blood stones – the largest ones ever discovered weighing 400 carats (80g/2.8 oz). Due to the political isolationism of the country that began in the seventies, good-sized Burmese rubies are now extremely hard to come by. Thailand and Sri Lanka have taken over supplying the market, but with stones of inferior quality. Because of its blood-like color, the ruby is a stone that traditionally represents vitality, and is meant to bring health and optimism to its owners. During the Middle Ages, alchemist physicians prescribed it as an antidote to venom and a cure for plague, and when placed on a wound, it was supposed to stop bleeding.

Opposite: Crocoite. Class: chromates (Tasmania).

Above: Faceted ruby weighing 5.04 carats (1.008g/0.036 oz). Class: oxides (Thailand).

1 Vanadinite. Class: vanadates (Morocco). 2 Fluorite. Class: halides (France). This crystal, housed in the National Museum of Natural History in Paris, is regarded as the finest specimen of fluorite in the world. 3 Rhodocrosite on quartz. Class: carbonates (USA). 4 Realgar. Class: sulphides (Peru). In Ancient times, the Chinese carved small decorative objects from realgar. These trinkets needed, however, to be handled with care, for realgar soon deteriorates when exposed to light, producing one of the deadliest poisons known to man – arsenic. 5 Rhodocrosite. Class: carbonates (South Africa). 6 Crocoite. Class: chromates (Tasmania).

Crocoite is a very rare stone, found in only two places in the world – the Urals and Tasmania – and its name is derived from the Greek *krokos,* meaning saffron, after its beautiful color. It was through his study of the first specimens to be found that the French chemist Nicolas Louis Vauquelin discovered chromium in 1797.

Opposite: Botryoidal rhodocrosite. Class: carbonates (Uruguay).

Following pages: Rhodocrosite with manganite. Class: carbonates (USA).

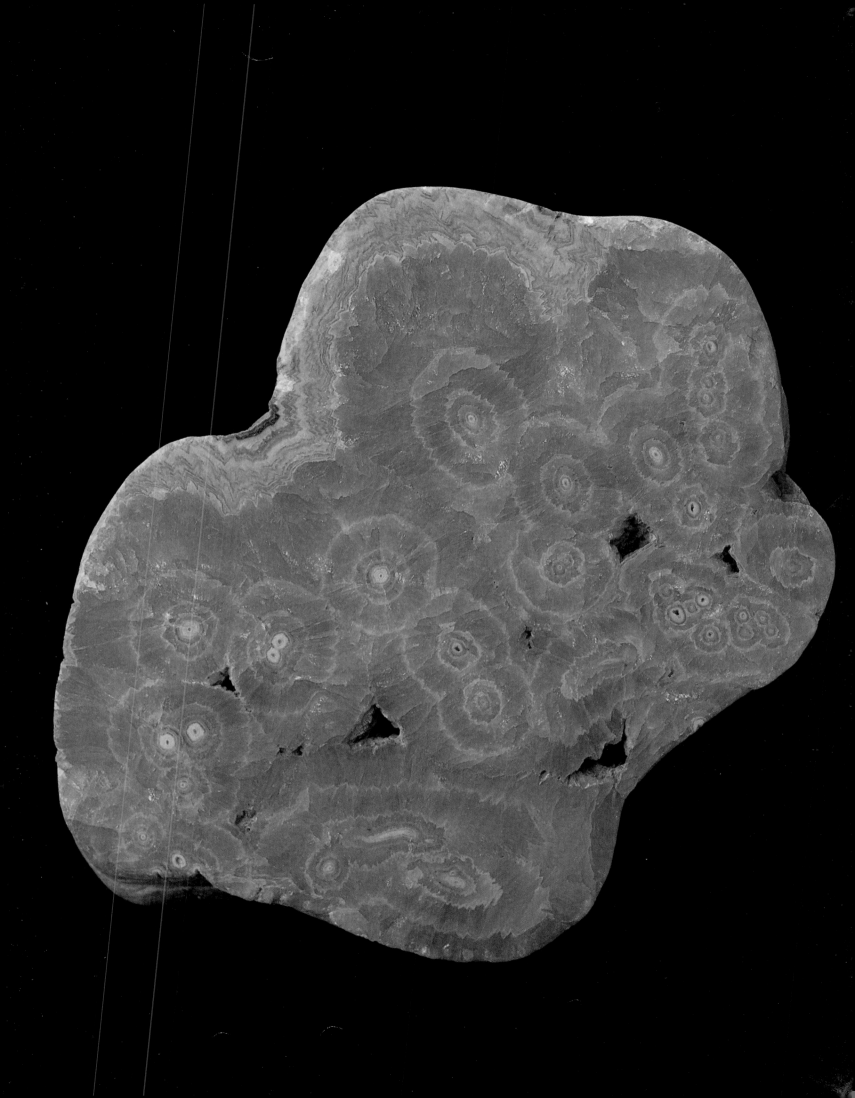

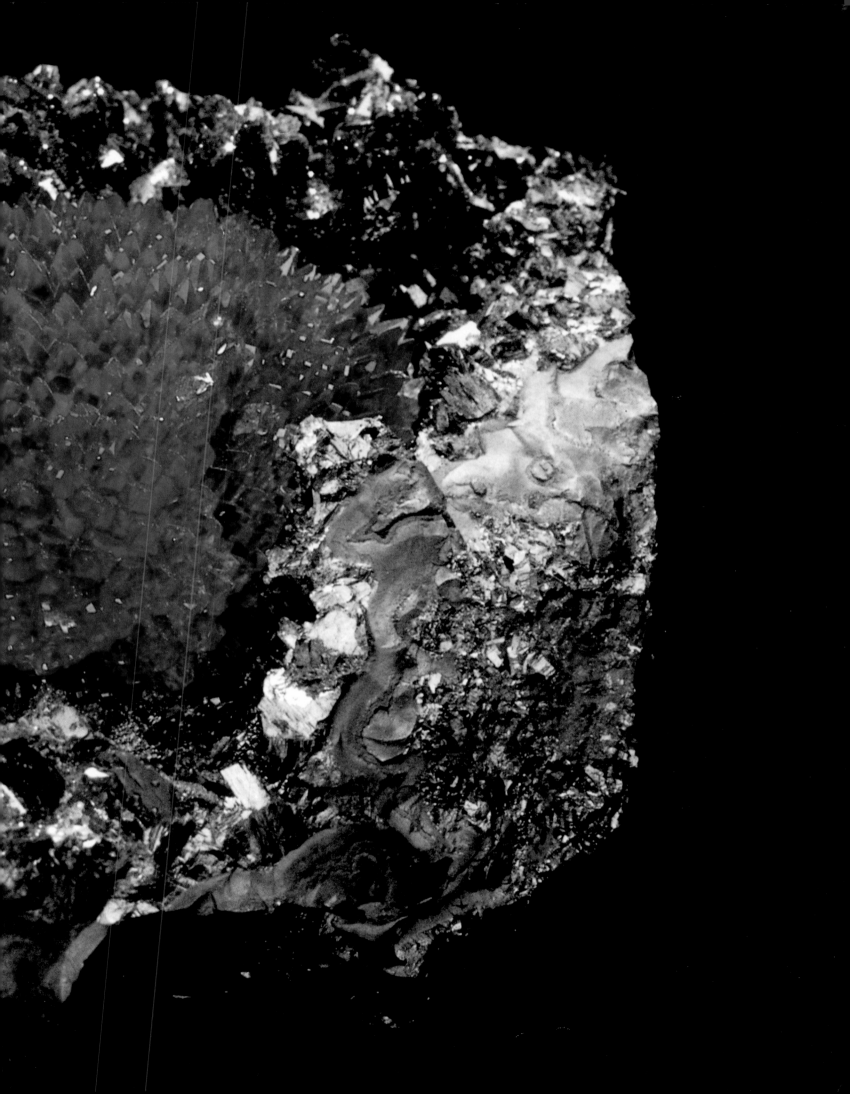

1 Rose quartz. Class: oxides (Brazil). **2** Rose quartz. Class: oxides (Madagascar). **3** Rhodocrosite. Class: carbonates (Uruguay). **4** Smithsonite. Class: carbonates (Mexico).

The Smithsonian Institute in Washington houses one of the finest mineral collections in the world, and the mineral smithsonite, found in widespread deposits on the American continent, is named after its founder, James Smithson (1765–1829). The practice of naming minerals after individuals, by adding the suffix *-ite,* dates only from the eighteenth century – previously, they had been named according to their appearance, shape or color. While this has sometimes led to less poetic names, it has resulted in a more structured nomenclature.

Opposite: Rhodocrosite on pyrite and quartz. Class: carbonates (Greece).

Before it first appeared in Europe, rhodocrosite was already familiar to the South American Indians, who used it for sculpting statuettes and for jewelery. It is still, in fact, known to jewelers as "rose of the Incas." Rhodocrosite is, however, valuable mainly as an important ore of manganese, used in the manufacture of special steel alloys.

1 Cobalto-calcite. Class: sulphides (Namibia). During the Middle Ages, the Scandinavians believed in mine-dwelling evil spirits called "metal demons," the most feared of whom caused explosions and noxious gases in the tunnels. Others, like the mischievous "kobolds" who created confusion by assuming the form of miners, were less harmful. This is the origin of the word cobaltite, a mineral commonly found in Sweden and Norway, where cobalt was discovered in the eighteenth century. 2 Quartz, cairngorm variety. Class: oxides. 3 Erythrite. Class: arsenates (Morocco). 4 Garnet. Class: silicates (Mexico). 5 Smithsonite. Class: carbonates (Mexico). 6 Spodumene, kunzite variety. Class: silicates (Afghanistan).

Minerals of the spodumene group are used chiefly in industry as a source of lithium. Only its transparent varieties, either pink (kunzite), green (hiddenite) or yellow in color, are prized as gemstones – despite the fact that its brittleness makes it a difficult stone to cut. Hiddenite, the rarest of the spodumenes, was discovered by an American farmer when he uprooted a tree.

Opposite: Smithsonite with pyrrhotite. Class: carbonates (Mexico).

Following pages: Pink beryl, morganite variety. Class: silicates (Brazil).

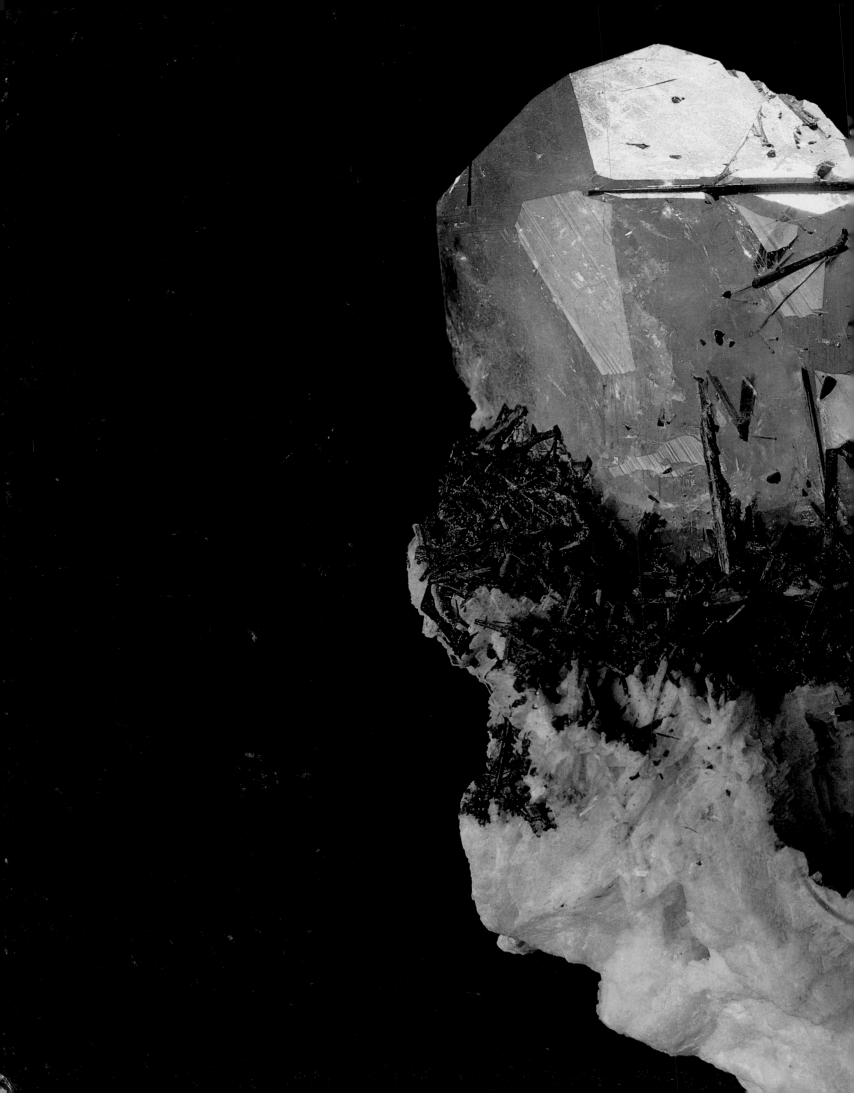

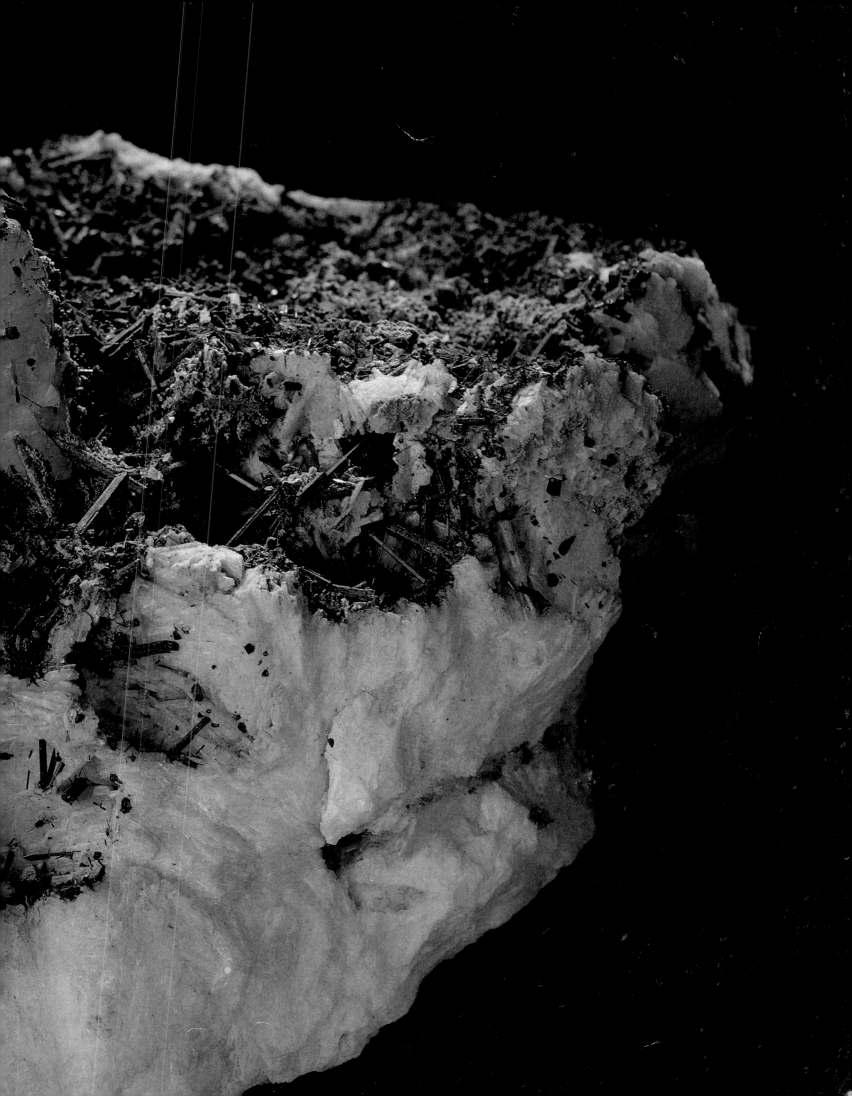

1 Rubellite tourmaline. Class: silicates. 2 Fluorite with grains of quartz. Class: halides (Spain). 3 Kammererite. Class: silicates (Turkey). 4 Erythrite. Class: arsenates (Morocco).

Erythrite sometimes occurs on rock in small pink clusters, earning it the name "cobalt bloom" (cobalt being the metal of which it is a compound). It is also valuable in that it can often indicate the presence of silver or uranium.

Opposite: Native arborescent copper. Class: elements (USA).

Copper was one of the earliest metals to be worked by man, with the oldest objects discovered dating from the sixth millennium BC. The naming of the period which saw the rise of metal-working as the "Copper Age" is evidence of copper's importance in the history of human civilization. Four millennia later, the invention of bronze by alloying copper with tin initiated further advances, and today copper ranks fourth in world mining production, its many uses including the manufacture of brass.

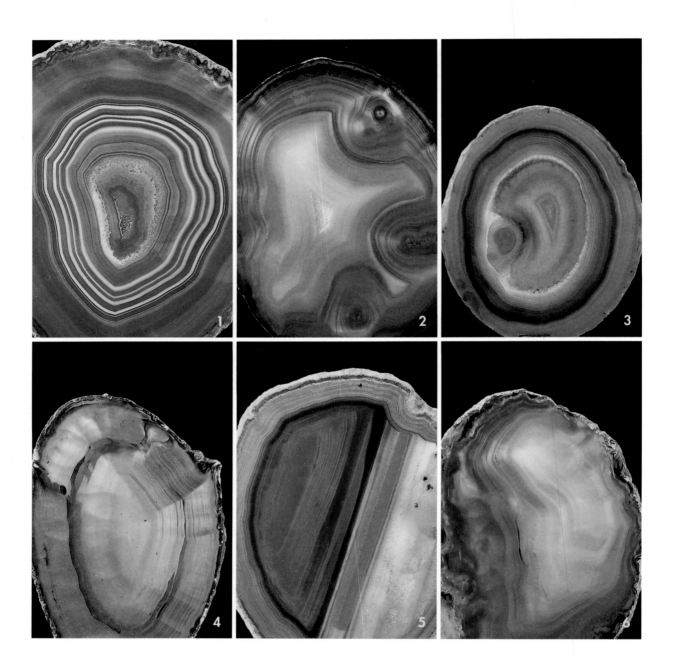

1 to **6** Minas Gerais agate. Class: oxides (Brazil).

Agate belongs to the large quartz group and is in fact chalcedony, formed in fine multi-colored layers from a small central crystal or around a foreign particle. According to legend, it was discovered in Sicily on the banks of the River Akhatês, hence the name "agate". Man has always been fascinated by the patterns that it traces. For example, an old poem attributed to Orpheus describes arborescent agate "like a flowering garden planted with numerous shrubs" – a characteristic that later led alchemists to think that it could help woodcutters to fell trees. It was invested with diverse magical powers. Peasants tied agate to their waists because they believed it assured them of a plentiful harvest. The Persians used agate fumigations to ward off lightning and storms. While it was used to treat the effects of snakebite, it was also, by contrast, meant to inflame feelings of love, as this ancient proverb illustrates: "Agate makes a man attractive to women who previously disliked him." When heated, agate can change color, forming onyx when black.

Opposite: Minas Gerais agate. Class: oxides (Brazil).

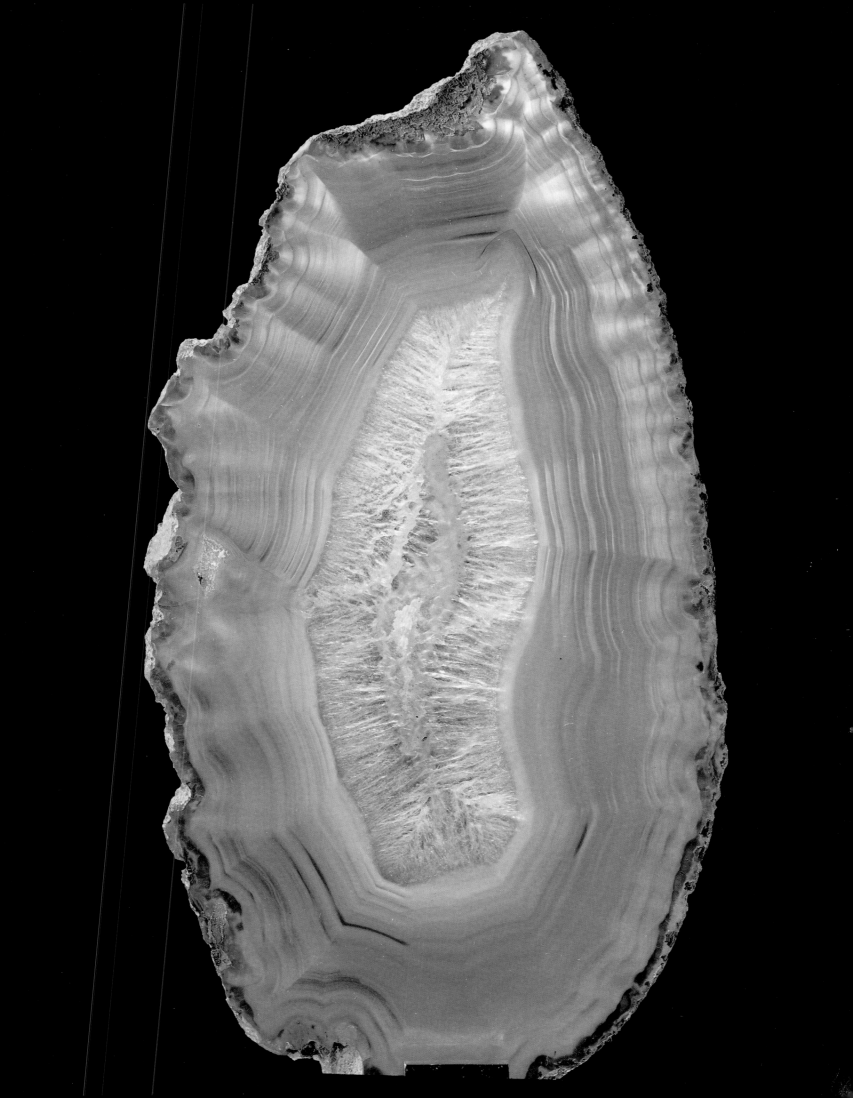

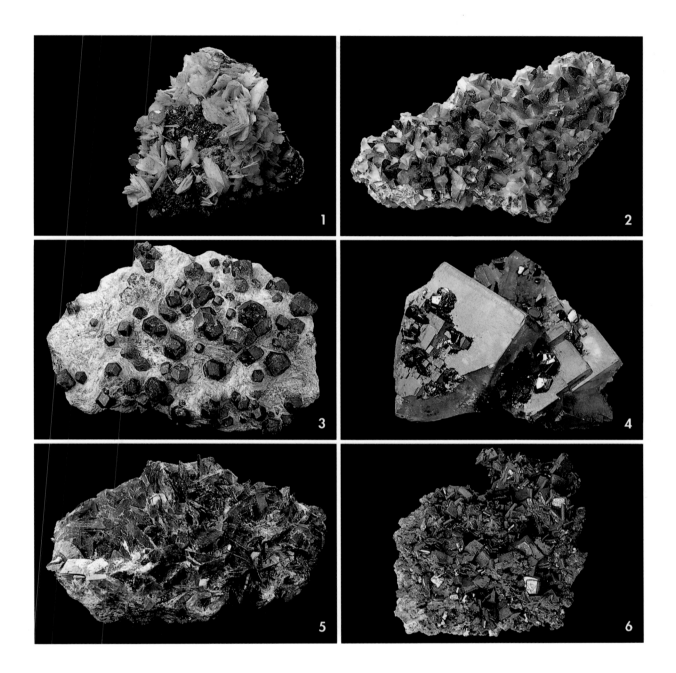

1 Barite with cerussite crystals. Class: sulphates (Morocco). 2 Calcite. Class: carbonates (Mexico). 3 Garnet, almandite variety. Class: silicates (Austria). 4 Fluorite and pitchblende. Class: halides (USA). 5 Axinite. Class: silicates (France). 6 Wulfenite. Class: molybdates (Mexico).

Opposite: Aragonite. Class: carbonates (Morocco).

Aragonite occurs in many different shapes, sometimes in unusual coral-like branches, hence the name "iron bloom." When used in the manufacture of decorative objects, it is known as "American onyx." Aragonite is also found in the nacre of both pearls and shells.

Following pages: Smoky quartz. Class: oxides (France).

1 Garnet. Class: silicates (France). 2 Vanadinite on goethite. Class: vanadates (Morocco). 3 Botryoidal haematite. Class: oxides (Great Britain). Prehistoric artists extracted a red pigment from haematite, using it most notably in the famous cave paintings at Lascaux, France, and it provides the "rouge indien" still used in industry for its resistance. It was once thought to be beneficial in the treatment of eye diseases and believed to bring victory to anyone taking it with them to a trial. Its blood-red color made it ideal for warriors who would rub it onto their skin before going into battle so as to save themselves from injury. 4 Zircon. Class: silicates (Brazil).

In Sri Lanka, zircon is panned from riverbed silt. When first removed from the water, the crystals are dull, but after cutting they take on a brilliance to rival diamond. Imitations are in fact made from it. Since blue zircon is the most sought after as a gemstone, many more common varieties are heated to turn them blue – an art whose secrets were jealously guarded for centuries by its Ceylonese masters. According to legend, zircon is the stone of Venus, and kindles a fire in the heart of its wearer. It is a source of two rare metals, zirconium and hafnium, which are today used in nuclear reactors.

Opposite: Smoky quartz. Class: oxides.

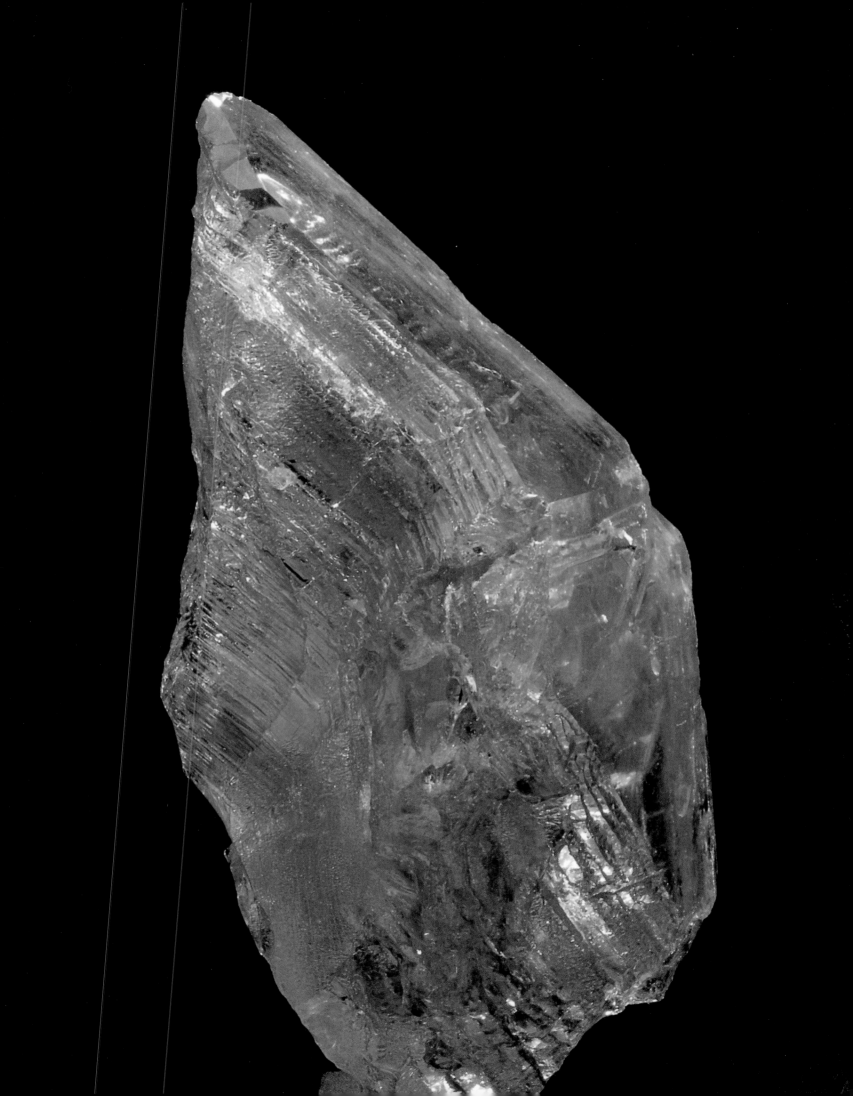

1 Botryoidal chalcedony. Class: oxides (France). 2 Quartz, variety: "cairngorm." Class: oxides (France).
3 Wulfenite and mimetite. Class: molybdates (Mexico). 4 Imperial topaz. Class: silicates (Brazil).
5 Wulfenite. Class: molybdates (Mexico). 6 Garnet. Class: silicates (Canada).

Opposite: Garnet. Class: silicates (Canada).

Garnet was among the most valued gemstones of the Middle Ages and derives its name from a corruption of the French *grenade*, meaning pomegranate, owing to their similarity of color. Pyrope has always been the most prized of the different varieties of garnet, with almandite worn as a talisman by the crusaders and the more orange-red spessartite given a place of honor at the court of King Clovis of France. Judging by the superb specimens unearthed accidentally during roadworks on 179th Street, it is thought that a major deposit of this last variety lies beneath Manhattan. The green demantoid variety, so called because of its diamond-like brilliance, is the rarest of the garnets and was discovered only as recently as 1868, by gold prospectors in the Urals. Garnet has long been believed to possess curative powers, especially in the treatment of melancholia, and because of its blood-like color, alchemist physicians thought it could ease complications during childbirth and stop bleeding. Some garnet crystals reach colossal sizes, like the staggering 700kg (1,543 lbs) specimen found in Norway.

1 Kammererite. Class silicates (Turkey). 2 Roselite. Class: arsenates (Morocco). 3 Purpurite. Class: phosphates (Namibia). 4 Garnet, grossularite variety. Class: silicates (Mexico). 5 Mimetite. Class: arsenates (Mexico). 6 Cinnabar (with mercury droplet). Class: sulphides (Spain).

Cinnabar was used in Ancient times as lipstick and its brilliant, vermilion-red pigment was highly prized by painters. Its principal significance, however, is as the chief ore of mercury. Simply tapping a piece of cinnabar will release a few droplets of the metal. Mercury is, in fact, the only metal that occurs as a liquid at normal temperature, solidifying only at -40°C (-104°F). As metals tend to resemble mercury when molten, alchemists believed mercury to be the basis of all metals. Mercury, therefore, came to be regarded as the precious element that could one day transform base metals into gold. Physicians used it to treat ailments of the nervous system for centuries and mercury salts remained the most widespread treatment for syphilis until the introduction of penicillin in 1941. Mercury is still used industrially in the manufacture of measuring apparatus such as thermometers and barometers.

Opposite: Vanadinite. Class: vanadates (Morocco).

Light and Shade

❏

Diamond is the queen of all gemstones. Reflecting yellows, greens and blues according to the play of light across the crystal, it is uniquely brilliant. Its origins have in the past been romantically attributed to stardust. Its composition, however, is of a more prosaic origin, being purely carbon, an element found in a baser form as coal and also as the graphite once used in the manufacture of pencil lead. Having noticed that neither heat nor tools could damage it, the Greeks called diamond *adamas*, meaning "invincible," the root of its modern name. As it is the hardest of all the minerals and can only be scratched by another diamond, gem-cutters use powdered diamond to facet the jewels. Its rarity also contributes to its value. On average, 250 metric tons (275 tons) of rock have to be mined to reveal a single gem-quality crystal which, when cut, rarely weighs more than one carat (0.2g/0.007 oz). For centuries, India was the only source of diamonds in the world. The spectacular deposits at Golconda, mined since the third millennium BC, provided the legendary jewels for royal crowns all over the world. Among the diamonds mined here was the legendary 108 carat "Koh-i-Noor," or "Mountain of Light," believed to possess the power of bringing world domination to its owner. Today it is the property of the British crown. In the eighteenth century, the diamond trade was transformed by the discovery of extensive deposits in Brazil and in Africa a century later. Remarkable specimens appeared, such as the "Cullinan," discovered in South Africa in 1905. It weighed 3106 carats (621g/22 oz) uncut, and over one hundred gems were cut from it, including the "Star of Africa" (530 carats,106g/3.7 oz), the largest faceted diamond in the world. Considering one 3 carat diamond is worth nearly a million dollars, these figures give pause for thought.

Opposite: Black fluorite.
Class: halides (Mexico).

Right: Pear cut diamond weighing 5.07 carats (1.014g/0.036 oz). Class: elements.

1 Iceland spar calcite. Class: carbonates (France). **2** Anglesite and galena. Class: sulphates (Morocco). **3** Cerussite. Class: carbonates (Morocco). **4** , **5** , **6** Hyaline quartz (rock crystal). Class: oxides (USA).

Together with the specimens of the feldspar group, quartz is the most widespread mineral on Earth and is found in sizes ranging from the microscopic particles of desert sand to enormous single crystals. When colorless, it is known as rock crystal, while its colored forms include such diverse varieties as amethyst (violet), citrine (yellow) and smoky quartz (brown). In Antiquity, quartz was believed to be water that had been turned to stone by severe cold, a view that persisted in Europe until the eighteenth century. The Greeks had learned that the sun could be used to ignite twigs or dried grass when its rays were focused through a piece of rock crystal. Priests were given sole charge of this "sacred fire" which they lit at important ceremonies. The idea that "petrified" water could create fire remained one of the greatest mysteries in ancient philosophy, leading to any number of magical properties being attributed to rock crystal. It became, most notably, the favored device of the soothsayers – hence the clairvoyant's familiar crystal ball. It was through perfecting the technique of melting quartz that the Egyptians invented glass, almost five thousand years ago.

Opposite: Smoky quartz. Class: oxides (France).

1 Grains of brookite on quartz. Class: oxides (Switzerland). **2** Quartz with pyrite. Class: oxides (Peru). **3** Quartz. Class: oxides (France). **4** , **5** , **6** Gypsum. Class: sulphates (France).

Opposite: Gypsum. Class: sulphates (France).

Gypsum belongs to the soft mineral group. It can easily be scratched, even with a fingernail, and has been worked by man from the earliest times. The Egyptians used it to make the sacred vases designed to contain the intestines of mummified bodies, while the Etruscans later carved gypsum bas-reliefs for their tombs. Its principal value is, however, economic, for when heated to between 150 and 200°C (305 and 390°F), gypsum is used to produce plaster – a process already known to the Egyptians by the third millennium BC. Huge gypsum quarries, dug for the plaster-manufacturing industry, grew beneath the streets of Paris for centuries. Some of these galleries became the catacombs, whereas others were converted into tunnels for the first lines of the Métro.

Following pages: Gypsum. Class: sulphates (Italy).

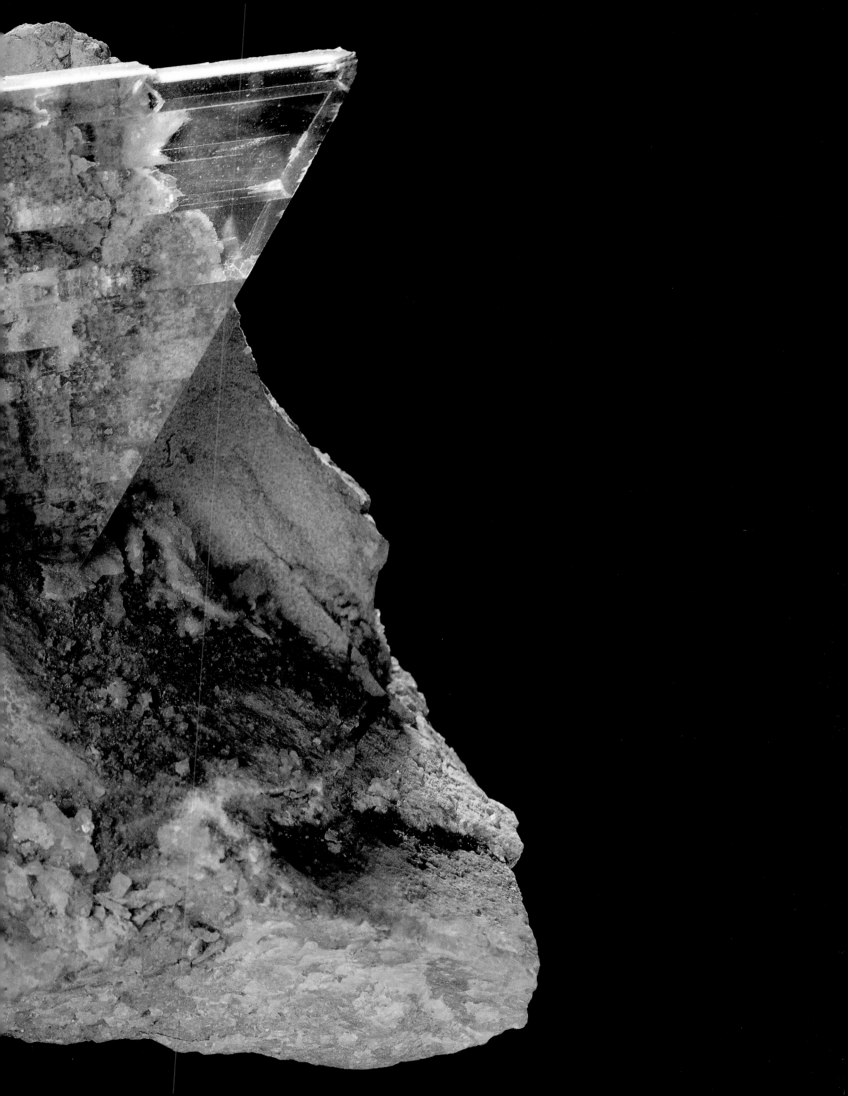

1 Hemimorphite. Class: silicates (Mexico). **2** Boulangerite. Class: sulphides (Romania). **3** Coating of white quartz on fluorite. Class: oxides (France). **4** Okenite. Class: silicates (India). **5** Stilbite. Class: silicates. **6** Sphalerite on calcite. Class: sulphides (France).

Hemimorphite and sphalerite are the two principal ores of zinc, a metal that man has known how to extract from its mineral sources only since the last century. It is cheap, has little tendency to rust, and is used chiefly to coat roofing materials. When alloyed with copper, it produces brass, also yielding an imitation silver used in costume jewelry when blended with nickel.

Opposite: Okenite. Class: silicates (India).

1 Galena with sphalerite. Class: sulphides (USA). **2** Vivianite. Class: phosphates (USA). **3** Galena and calcite. Class: sulphides (USA).
4 Molybdenite. Class: molybdates (Australia). **5** Galena on sphalerite. Class: sulphides (Peru).
6 Octahedral galena. Class: sulphides (France).

Galena is both the most economically important ore of lead and one of the principal ores of silver. In the early days
of wireless communication, galena crystals were used in radio receivers.

Opposite: Huebnerite with quartz. Class: tungstates (Peru).

1 Fluorite. Class: halides (France). 2 Quartz spray. Class: oxides (France). 3 Aragonite. Class: carbonates (Mexico). 4 Dolomite. Class: carbonates (Spain). 5 Dovetail gypsum. Class: sulphates (Mexico). 6 Quartz. Class: oxides (USA).

Opposite: Rock salt (halite). Class: halides (Poland).

Along with flint, salt was one of the first commodities to be sold. It has been of crucial importance since prehistoric times, for in addition to serving as a condiment, it can be used to preserve meat and cauterize wounds. In many ancient civilizations, including Egypt, the salt industry was a state monopoly – a practice that persisted in France until the eighteenth century, with the levy of a royal salt tax called the *gabelle*. As it prevents dehydration, salt is vital to the survival of desert peoples and was long used as currency by nomads, for whom it was more precious than gold. The world's most extraordinary salt mines are found at Wieliczka in Poland, where miners have carved a long series of statues and bas-reliefs in the salt seams dozens of meters below ground. None of these masterpieces can be brought to the surface, as the humidity in the air would destroy them instantly.

Following pages: Dolomite. Class: carbonates (Spain).

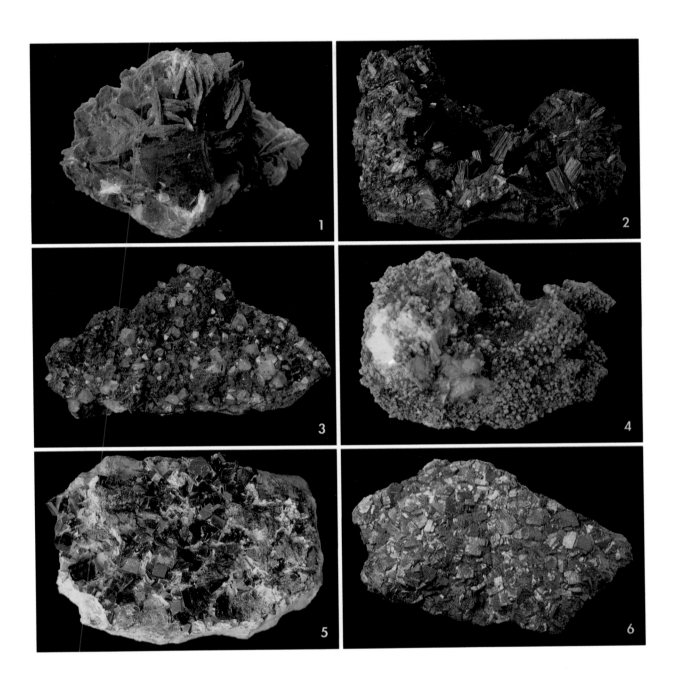

1 Fluorite with barite. Class: halides (France). **2** Manganite. Class: oxides (Germany). **3** Cerussite. Class: carbonates (Morocco). **4** Boulangerite. Class: sulphides (France). **5** Siderite on calcite. Class: carbonates (Brazil). **6** Haematite. Class: oxides (France).

Opposite: Fluorite with barite. Class: halides (France).

1 Barite with grain of galena. Class: sulphates (France). **2** Barite. Class: sulphates (Romania). **3** Aragonite. Class: carbonates. **4** Kaolinite with quartz. Class: silicates (France). Kaolinite is the main constituent of kaolin, a white and crumbly rock used in the manufacture of ceramics and porcelain, hence the name "China clay." **5** Prehnite. Class: silicates (India). **6** Dolomite on sphalerite. Class: carbonates (Yugoslavia).

Opposite: Asbestos serpentine. Class: silicates (Canada).

The term asbestos covers different varieties of fibrous minerals that are particularly resistant to fire – hence its name which in Greek means "incombustible."

Following pages: Arsenic with rammelsbergite. Class: elements (France).

Native arsenic is most commonly found in loosely-shaped aggregates, volatilizing when heated and producing a strong garlicky smell. It is not dangerous in itself, but the compound arsenic trioxide is highly poisonous and milk is believed to be the best antidote for it.

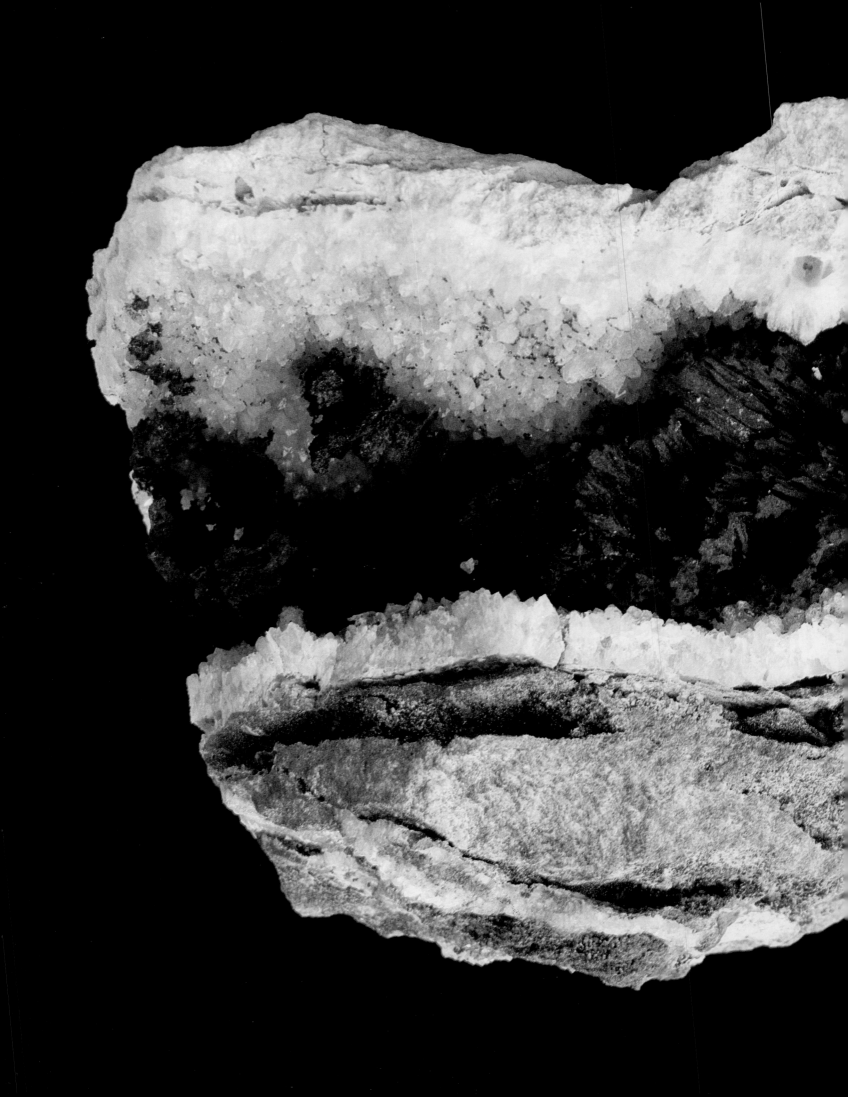

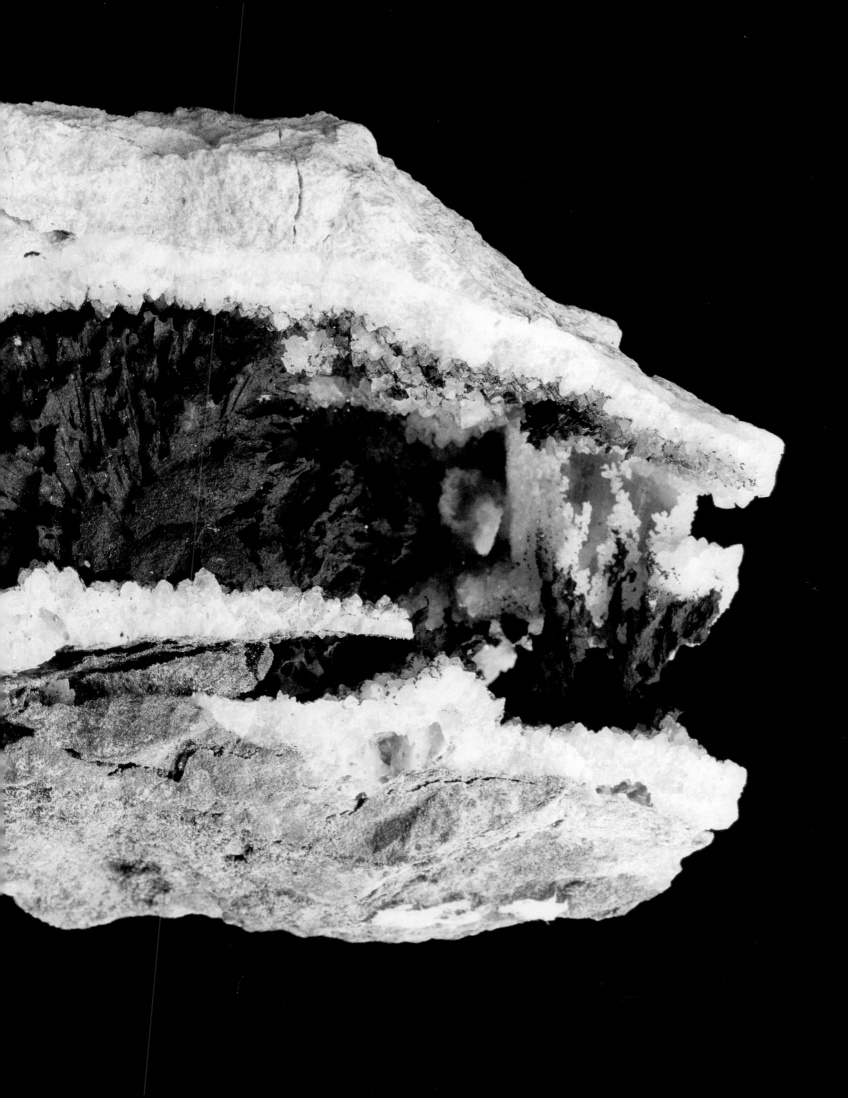

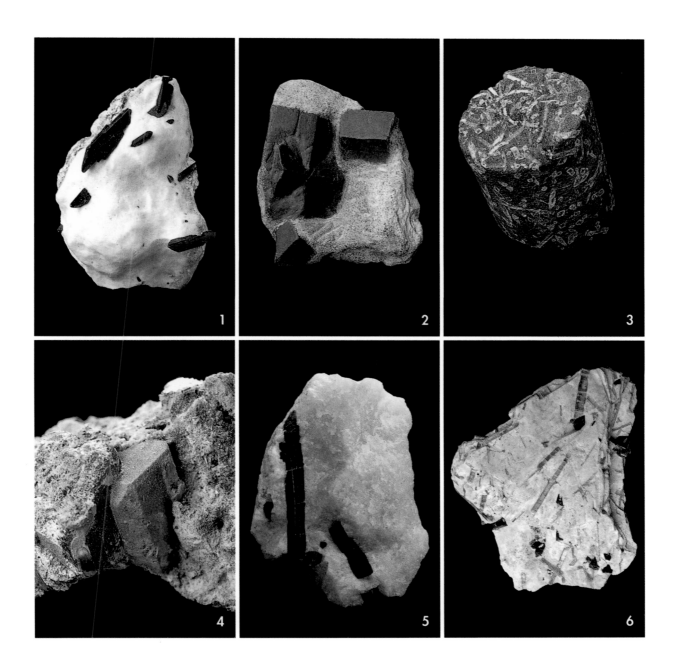

1 Neptunite. Class: silicates (USA). 2 Staurolite. Class: silicates (France). 3 Andalusite. Class: silicates (France). 4 Phosgenite. Class: carbonates (Italy). 5 Tourmaline, variety "schorl," in quartz. Class: silicates (France). 6 Staurolite encrusted in cyanite. Class: silicates (Switzerland).

Opposite: Staurolite. Class: silicates (France).

Staurolite crystals are often twinned in strange cruciform shapes – a characteristic that made a strong impression on Christian Europe. There are many legends that link it to the Holy Cross, attributing to it such miraculous properties as the power to treat diseases of the eye, cure madness and protect against rabid animals. It is sometimes used to make rosary beads, and in the region around Baud and Coray in Brittany, northern France, where it is particularly common, it was believed to prevent shipwreck. While some staurolites are not so characteristically cruciform, they have nevertheless been traditionally venerated in the same way. An old Breton song explains that some represent the cross and others the nails and the thorns of Christ's crown.

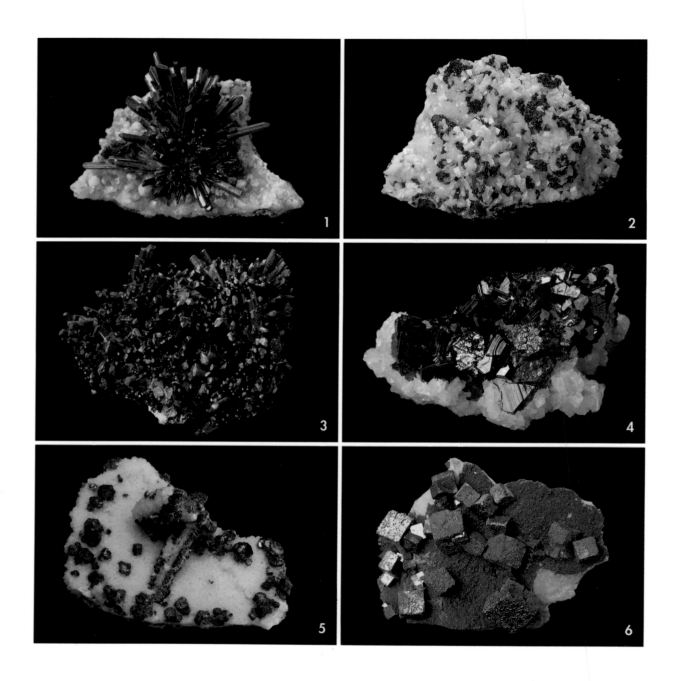

1 Stibnite on quartz. Class: sulphides (Romania). 2 Dolomite with sphalerite. Class: carbonates (France). 3 Stibnite. Class: sulphides (Romania). 4 Sphalerite on calcite. Class: sulphides (Yugoslavia). 5 Tennantite with quartz. Class: sulphides (USA). 6 Galena. Class: sulphides (USA).

Opposite: Black quartz, "morion" variety. Class: oxides (France).

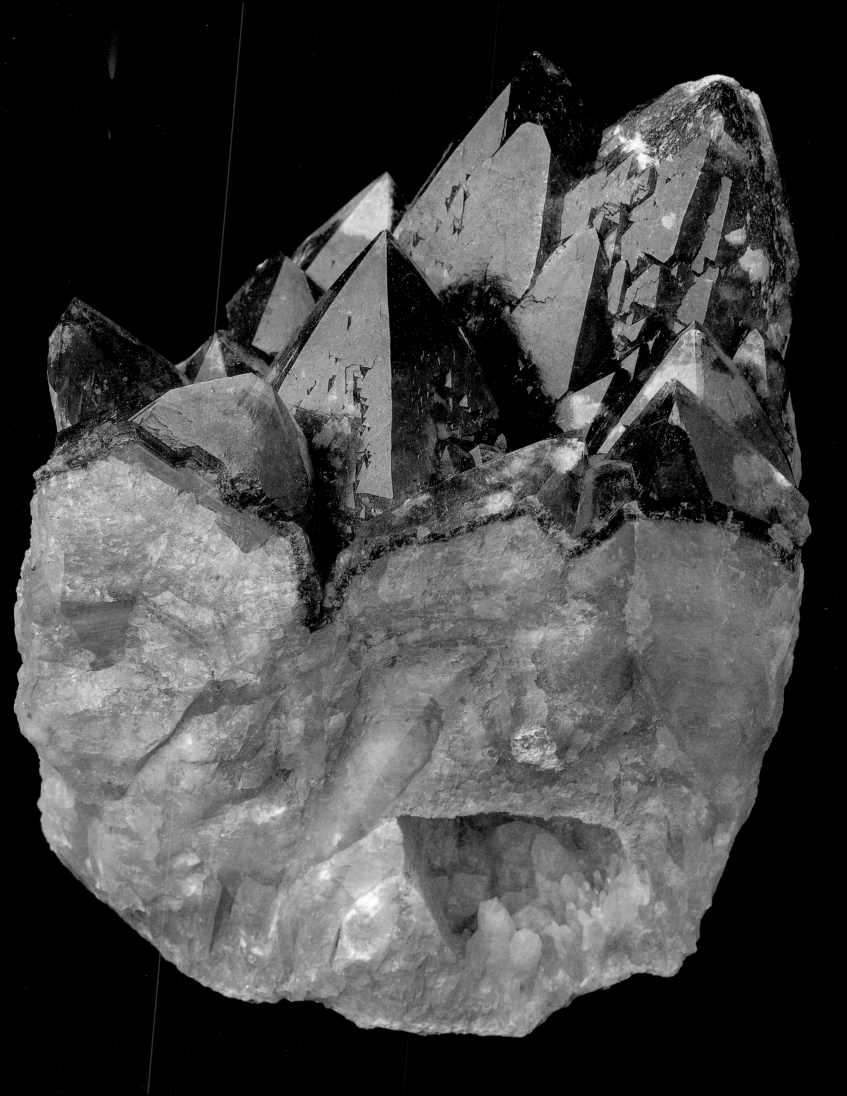

1 Arsenopyrite (mispickel). Class: sulphides (Portugal). 2 Molybdenite in quartz. Class: molybdates (USA). 3 Schorl tourmaline with albite and mica on orthoclase. Class: silicates (Brazil). 4 Bournonite on quartz. Class: sulphides (Romania). 5 Chalcedony, "lussatite" variety. Class: oxides (France). 6 Axinite. Class: silicates (Russia).

Opposite: Barite with fluorite and galena on sphalerite. Class: sulphates (USA).

Following pages: Magnetite. Class: oxides (USA).

Certain varieties of magnetite can attract iron, hence the name "lodestone." It was known to the Greeks around 400 BC and was rubbed on the skin to treat illness – the origin of "magnetic therapy" still practised today. Dioscorides, a Greek physician of the first century AD, advised any suspicious husband to secretly place lodestone in his bed. If his wife were faithful, she would kiss him immediately; should her conduct have been less than irreproachable, the lodestone would cause her to fall out of bed! During the Middle Ages, magnetite was highly valued by alchemists, being a constituent of the philosophers' stone that was believed to facilitate the transformation of base metals into gold. Lodestone is still used in the electronics industry, chiefly in the manufacture of radio and television sets.

1 Haematite. Class: oxides (France). 2 Tantalite. Class: oxides (Madagascar). 3 Haematite. Class: oxides (Brazil).
4 Galena. Class: sulphides (USA). 5 Wolframite. Class: tungstates (Portugal). 6 Botryoidal marcasite. Class: sulphides (France).

As their chemical composition is similar and they often occur together, marcasite was long confused with pyrite. To add to the confusion, Marcasite's name is derived from the Old Arabic *marchesita,* meaning pyrite. Attractive as it may be, marcasite can pose problems for the collector – as it oxidizes it produces sulphuric acid which attacks the wood of the collecting cabinet and can even damage minerals placed close to it.

Opposite: Enargite. Class: sulphides (Taiwan).

Unusual Minerals

❏

Each year, approximately 20,000 metric tons (22,046 tons) of meteorites enter the atmosphere and fall to Earth. While the vast majority are made up of "cosmic dust," tiny particles that measure only millimeters across, giant meteorites, measuring ten kilometers (6.2 miles) or more in diameter, do not belong purely to the realms of apocalyptic science fiction. Scientists calculate that one of these meteors is highly likely to collide with our planet, but only once in every 40 million years. An object of this size, traveling at a speed of 20 kilometers (12.4 miles) per second, would have an impact one thousand times more powerful than the atomic bomb detonated at Hiroshima, and it is now thought that such a meteorite may have led to the extinction of the dinosaurs. Unlike the Earth, the moon has no atmosphere to protect it. Its familiar craters are the scars left by enormous meteorites, some of which have produced depressions over 100 kilometers (62 miles) long. Since the earliest times, man's·fears and superstitions have featured "stones that drop from the sky." The Gauls' fear that the sky would one day collapse on their heads may have been linked to the recollection of such an object falling from space. The famous black stone at Mecca is thought to be a meteorite that fell to Earth long before the foundation of Islam. Research into meteorites is vital to an understanding of our origins. Created at the same time as the solar system itself, billions of years ago, they constitute a rich, primeval source of information as to the evolution of our own planet.

Opposite: Landscape sandstone (USA).

Left: Part of a meteorite that fell to Earth in 1751.

1 Fossil (*Lescuropteris genuina*). **2** Fossil (*Dicksonites sterzeli*). **3** Fossil (*Odontopteris minor-zeilleri*). **4** Fossil (*Pecopteris arborescens*). **5** Fossil (*Knorria*). **6** Fossil (*Taeniopteris multinervis*).

Fossils are the traces of animals or plants preserved in rock. Many are in fact casts, as the mineral substance that initially covered them has ended up taking their place. The oldest organism ever discovered is a bacterium, a form of marine plant dating from three billion years ago. Many now extinct species are, like this one, known to us only from their mineral remains. It is the study of fossils that enables palaeontologists to piece together the links in the great chain of evolution.

Opposite: Fossil (*Encrinus liliiformis*).

Echinoderm fossils are the subject of intensive research, for it has now been suggested that these organisms are the ancestors of the vertebrates. This echinoderm, a distant relative of the sea urchin, evolved in the depths of the sea around 220 million years ago.

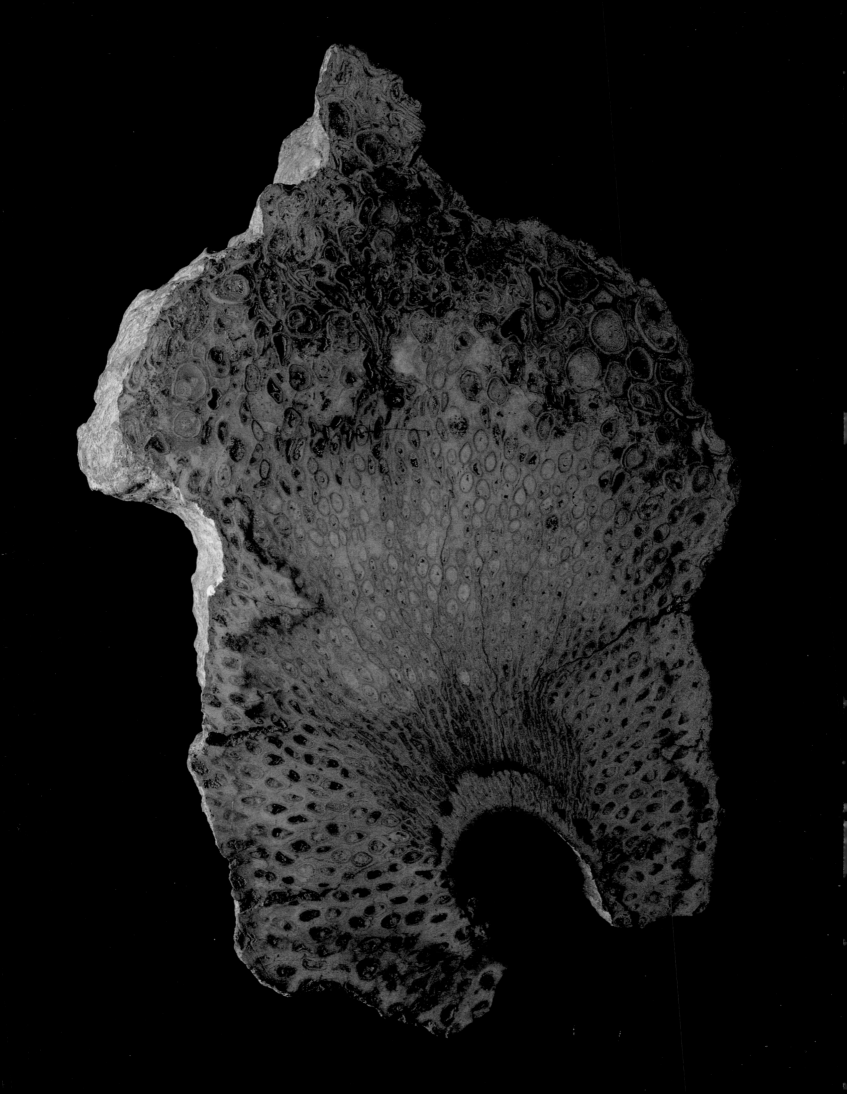

1 Fossil *(Psaronius bibractensis).* **2** Fossil *(Colpoxylon aedvense).* **3** Fossilized walnut tree from Deux-Sèvres, France (60cm/24 in). **4** Fossilized vine leaves. **5** Petrified sequoia from Arizona (110cm/43 in). When wood is petrified by jasper or chalcedony, it naturally joins the category of semiprecious stones. The most famous specimens are the sequoias of the Petrified Forest National Monument near Holbrook, Arizona, some of which are 30m (98.4 ft) in length. **6** Fossilized palm leaf.

Opposite: Fossil *(Psaronius augustodunensis).*

Following pages: Fossilized crocodile (56m/184 ft).

Crocodileimus robustus lived around 140 million years ago and is known to us only by this perfectly preserved fossil, discovered in limestone deposits near Cerin, in the Ain department of France. In Germany, in 1861, it was again limestone that yielded the fossilized remains of *Archaeopteryx,* which lived 150 million years ago and is the ancestor of birds. The fossil enabled scientists to show that birds were descended from reptiles, or rather dinosaurs, to be precise.

1 Fossil *(Memre rhombeus)*. **2** Actinopterygian fossil. **3** Fossilized shark's tooth. **4** Fossilized fish *(Dapedius pholidotus)*. **5** Fossilized fish *(Furo praelongus)*. **6** Ammonite fossil.

Opposite: Fossilized mollusc *(Harpoceras toarcien)*.

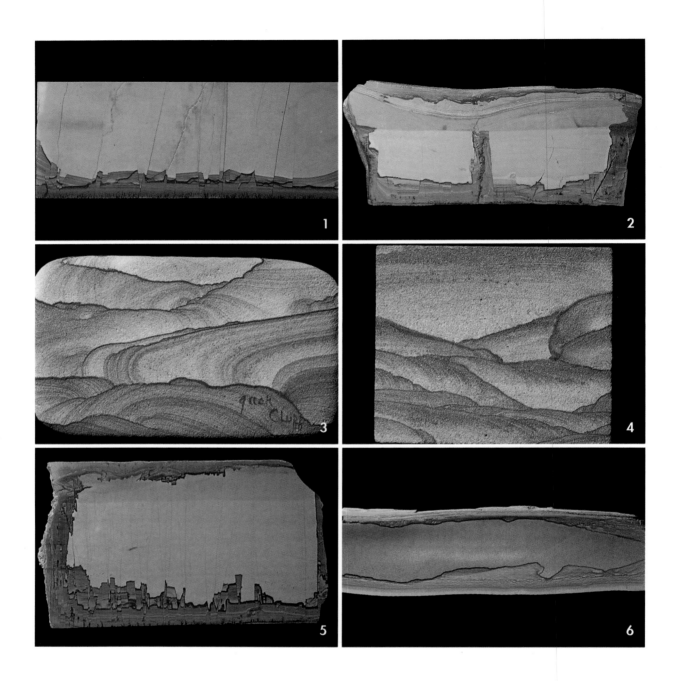

1 Landscape limestone (Italy). 2 Landscape limestone (Italy). 3 Landscape sandstone (signed "Jack Cluff") (USA). 4 Landscape sandstone (USA). 5 Landscape limestone (Italy). 6 Landscape limestone (Italy).

The permeation of iron or manganese into rocks can sometimes create intriguing patterns that suggest the abstract quality of Japanese art or the exuberant vitality of Impressionism. As early as the Renaissance, painters had developed a fondness for embellishing these landscape minerals, adding decorative details here and there which nature had inadvertently neglected. The American artist Jack Cluff simply polished landscape sandstones that he found while out walking, then signed them to make the picture complete. Landscape minerals that resemble people are highly sought after by collectors and some can fetch up to $5,000.

Opposite: Landscape sandstone with dendritic manganese oxide.

Following pages: Landscape limestone.

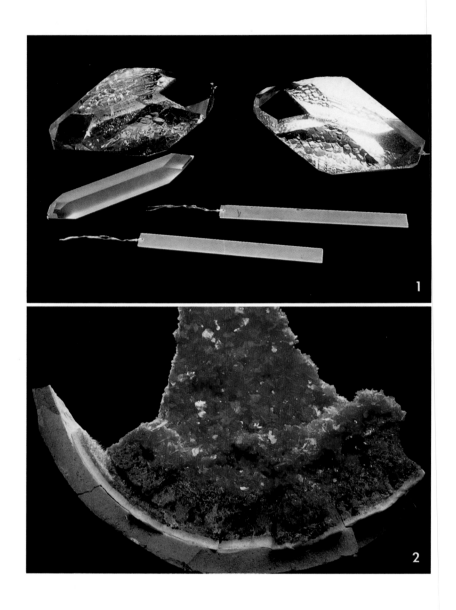

1 Quartz (artificially grown crystals). **2** Synthetic rubies.

For thousands of years, man has known how to alter the appearance of stones so as to make them more beautiful and therefore more valuable. The use of heat is one of the oldest techniques, causing the color of certain minerals to change. When skilfully heated, a yellow corundum can, for example, turn blue as a sapphire, but collectors regard these specimens as a poor substitute for the real thing. New horizons have been opened up – it is now possible to create in a matter of weeks what nature has taken millions, even billions, of years to produce. Synthetic stones are not mere imitations, but authentic minerals whose appearance and chemical composition are identical in every way to their natural counterparts. The majority of hyaline quartz used in industry (chiefly in watch-making) is in fact manufactured from simple saline solutions in an autoclave. Precious stones are not exempt from this process – the first to be synthetically produced was the ruby, in 1891. Although these can often better natural rubies in brilliance and size, they are nowhere near as valuable, costing on average five hundred times less. Owing to their considerable hardness, their uses are mainly industrial. Many gemstones, including emerald, sapphire and even the precious diamond, are now synthetically manufactured.

Opposite: Gypsum (artificially grown crystals).

1 and **2** White hydrozincite (blue fluorescence). Class: carbonates (Mexico). **3** Brown chalcedony (green fluorescence).
Class: oxides (Brazil).
5 Green fluorite (violet fluorescence). Class: halides (Great Britain). **4** and **6** Yellow autunite (green fluorescence).
Class: phosphates (France).

When exposed to ultraviolet light or X-rays, certain minerals display a strange luminescence, causing an apparent change of color. This phenomenon is known as fluorescence, so called because it was first observed in fluorite. Diamond and ruby also display this characteristic, though it in no way affects their value as gemstones. When this luminescence continues after the light source has been turned off, the phenomenon is known as phosphorescence.

Opposite: Brazilian jasper.

The color of a mineral is closely associated with its chemical composition. Thus, the colors blue and green often indicate the presence of copper in the basic formula, red and black that of iron, yellow that of uranium, and so on.

177

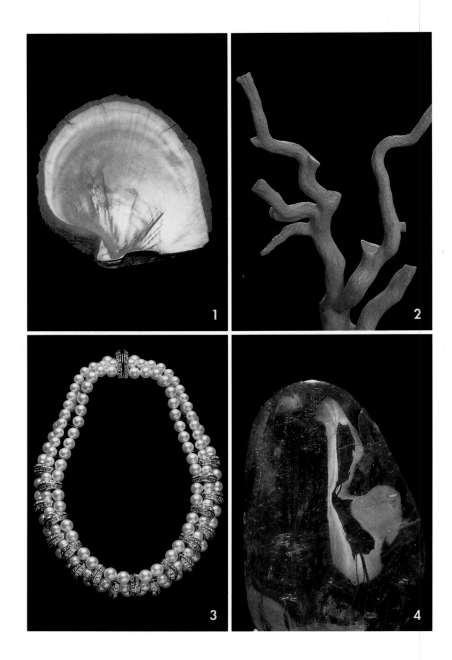

1 Mother-of-pearl from the Philippines. **2** Mediterranean coral. **3** Pearl necklace set with diamonds. **4** Baltic amber.

Solid substances produced naturally by certain living organisms are as much prized for making precious objects as are the finest gemstones. The pearls of molluscs, such as the oyster, and the nacre of shells are in fact composed of aragonite. Coral is the calcareous secretion produced by microscopic marine organisms called polyps, close relatives of the jellyfish.

Opposite: Amber from the Dominican Republic (30 million years old).

Amber is not a rock, but a fossilized resin exuded by trees in the vast coniferous forests that grew on Earth fifty million years ago. Minute insects often became trapped, and subsequently fossilized, within it. The Greeks observed that by rubbing it vigorously with a cloth, amber would attract particles of dust. They called it *élektron*, hence the name "electricity" later given to this form of energy.

Following pages: Giant quartz crystals (weighing 500kg/1,102 lbs each). Class: oxides (Brazil).

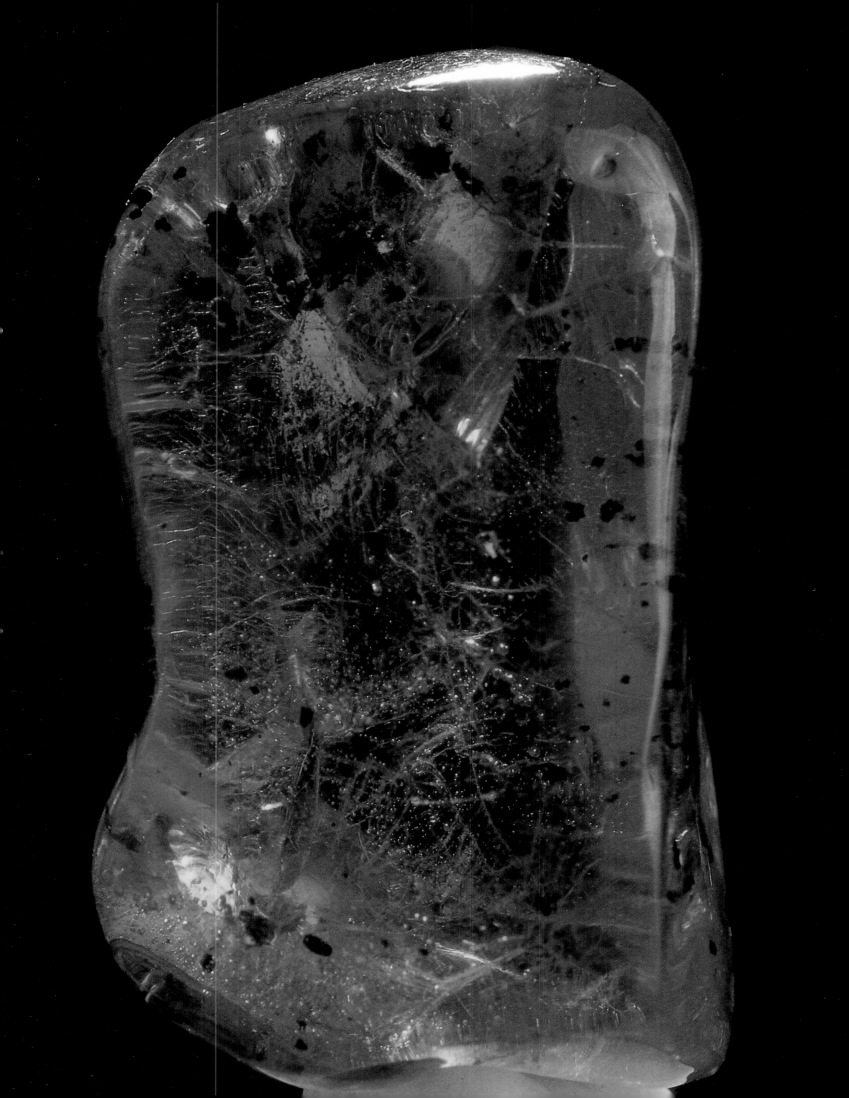

Glossary

❏

Aggregate: irregular mass of crystals.

Carat: unit of weight used for gemstones equal to 0.2g (0.007 oz). The word is derived from the Arabic *quirat,* meaning "carob"; as the seeds of this fruit have a constant weight (0.2g), the Arabs adopted them for weighing gemstones. When applied to gold, the carat is a measure of purity, not weight, indicating the proportion of pure gold contained in an alloy (24 carats for pure gold, 12 carats for an alloy containing 50% gold, etc.).

Carbonates (nitrates and borates): carbonates are the salts (q.v.) of carbonic acid and are traditionally grouped with nitrates (the salts of nitric acid) and borates (the salts of boric acid). Minerals in this class number 314 and are generally soft, some being water-soluble.

Cleavage: striking a mineral causes it to break in different ways, dependent upon its crystalline structure, and the word cleavage is applied to regular patterns of breakage. Whether they are observed with a magnifying glass or under the microscope, the shapes obtained are always geometrically identical. For example, breaking diamond always produces shapes with eight faces. Cleavage is described as perfect when a mineral cleaves readily. Some minerals have no cleavage, such as metals, which are malleable. When the breakage is irregular,

with no defined geometrical shape, it is called a fracture (as in the case of glass).

Crystal: faceted, geometrical shape assumed naturally by minerals as they solidify, provided that nothing impedes their growth. The word was first applied to colorless quartz (rock crystal) but has since been extended to cover all minerals.

Crystalline structure: minerals differ from liquids and gases in the rigidly symmetrical disposition of their atoms. The formation of the atoms into an initially microscopic molecule creates the building block from which a future crystal grows. The symmetrical habit then determines the way in which the faces of the crystal develop, with an infinite number of additional blocks, each having an identical structure, added to the first until a complete crystal is formed. There are seven different crystal systems, classified according to the symmetrical habit of the atoms: cubic; tetragonal (an elongated cube); hexagonal (a prism with a hexagonal base); rhombohedral (a parallelepiped with rhomboidal faces); orthorhombic (a perpendicular prism with a rhomboidal base); monoclinic (a non-perpendicular prism with a rhomboidal base); and triclinic (a prism with unequal axes and angles). The forms of all classified minerals stem from these simple shapes.

Density: the mass of a substance relative to the mass of water – a mineral with a density of 5 has a mass five times greater than the equivalent volume of water. Metals are the densest minerals, with densities of 21.5 for platinum and 19.3 for gold.

Ductile: (of a metal) that which can be drawn into wire, such as silver, gold, etc.

Halides: minerals composed of a metallic element combined with a halogen (the halogens being fluorine, chlorine, bromine and iodine). Minerals in this small class (there are less than 150 recorded) are often water-soluble with a salty taste, and the name halide is taken from the Greek *halos,* meaning cooking salt.

Hardness: a mineral's resistance to scratching. A scale of hardness is used (called the Mohs scale, after its inventor), ranging from 1 (for talc) to 10 (for diamond). Any mineral with a hardness of below 2.5 can be scratched with a fingernail.

Inclusion: presence of a solid, gaseous or liquid material inside a crystal.

Lustre: the brilliance of a mineral when exposed to light. The terms used to describe lustre include: metallic (specific to metals and sulphides); adamantine (having the sharp brilliance of diamond); vitreous (glassy); greasy (less sharp than adamantine or vitreous lustres, owing to fissures on the surface of the crystal); resinous (applied to yellow minerals, whose lustre is similar to that of a resin); pearly (applied to minerals whose fissured crystals produce an iridescent effect); silky (applied to fibrous minerals); waxy; and earthy or dull (applied to minerals like talc, which occur in fine aggregates).

Malleable: (of a metal) that which can be hammered flat without being damaged (e.g., gold, copper, etc.).

Mineral: a pure or compound chemical substance occurring naturally as a solid. Minerals either occur alone in the Earth's crust or combine to form rocks (q.v.).

Native element: a pure, chemically un-combined substance that occurs in nature as a solid. The term covers all the metals (e.g., gold, silver, platinum, copper, iron, mercury, etc.), their characteristics being malleability, high density, lack of cleavage and metallic lustre. Closely related to the metals are the semi-metals (arsenic, antimony, bismuth, etc.), which are generally less malleable, and the non-metals (sulphur, carbon, etc.), which by contrast are brittle, have low density and no metal lustre. The class of native elements numbers 101 members, including various metal alloys.

Ore: rock or mineral containing one or more elements (usually a metal) whose extraction is economically viable. The determining factor here is profitability – an iron-bearing mineral is only an ore if the iron can be extracted profitably.

Oxides (and hydroxides): when combined with oxygen, metals become oxides – the precious metals, apart from silver, are the only exceptions to the rule. Whereas iron oxide produces rust, aluminium oxide can form ruby or sapphire. The term hydroxide is applied to the combination of a metal with hydrogen. The class numbers 517 minerals.

Phosphates (arsenates and vanadates): phosphates are the salts (q.v.) of phosphoric acid, producing soft and often richly colored minerals of varying density. They are traditionally grouped with the arsenates (which are the salts of arsenic acid), and the vanadates (the salts of vanadic acid). The class numbers 632 minerals.

Rock: building material of the Earth's crust and composed of one or more minerals.

Salt: in chemistry, an acid is a compound of hydrogen, oxygen and one other element; e.g., carbon in carbonic acid, or phosphorous in phosphoric acid. When the acid reacts with a metal, the hydrogen of the acid is replaced by the metal, producing what is called a salt. These salts form the basis of a great many minerals.

Silicates: class of minerals whose basic component is silicon combined with oxygen (i.e., silicon oxide), numbering 916 species which make up 95% of the Earth's crust. The complexity of the minerals in the class has led to the silicates being sub-divided according to their crystalline structure, rather than their chemical formula, into the following groups: independent tetrahedral silicates; double tetrahedral silicates; ring silicates; single-chain silicates; double-chain silicates; sheet silicates; and framework silicates.

Streak: powdery trace left by a mineral when rubbed across a plate. The color of the streak is a useful, additional method of identifying a mineral and can sometimes vary from that of the crystal.

Sulphates (chromates, molybdates and tungsates): sulphates are the salts (q.v.) of sulphuric acid, their principal constituent being sulphur. Minerals in this class are soft, transparent or translucent when pure, or else faintly colored, and sometimes water-soluble. They are usually grouped with the chromates (which are the salts of chromic acid), the molybdates (the salts of molybdic acid) and the tungstates (the salts of tungstic acid). The class numbers 316 minerals.

Sulphides (and sulphosalts): class of minerals composed of one or more metallic elements in combination with sulphur (galena, for example, is a compound of lead and sulphur). The sulphur may be replaced by a related element, such as arsenic or antimony — providing the arsenides and the antimonides. The term sulphosalt is applied when the basic formula combines these elements with sulphur (tennantite, for example, is a compound of copper, iron and sulphur to which arsenic has also been added). The 539 minerals in this class include many ores.

Tenacity: a mineral's structural resistance – not to be confused with hardness, which is a measure of surface resistance. Although diamond is the hardest mineral, it displays brittleness if an attempt is made to cut through it and is therefore described as having low tenacity.

Transparency: a mineral is described as transparent when it is possible to see through its crystal, translucent when the crystal merely filters the light and opaque when no light can pass through it. A crystal's transparency determines whether it qualifies as a gemstone.

Twinning: joining of two or more crystals in a regular arrangement (staurolite often occurs in twinned cruciform crystals).

Mineralogical classification of the minerals featured

CLASS	MINERAL	VARIETY	PRINCIPAL ELEMENTS	DENSITY	HARDNESS	LUSTRE	TRANSPARENCY	COLOR	CRYSTAL SYSTEM
Native elements	Arsenic		arsenic	5.7	3.5	metallic	opaque	grey	R
	Copper		copper	8.9	2.5	metallic	opaque	red	C
	Diamond		carbon	3.5	10	adamantine	transparent, opaque	colorless, yellow	C
	Gold		**gold**	19.3	3	metallic	opaque	yellow	C
	Mercury		**mercury**	13.5	liquid	metallic	opaque	white	/
	Platinum		**platinum**	21.5	4.5	metallic	opaque	grey	C
	Silver		silver	10.5	3	metallic	opaque	white	C
	Sulphur		**sulphur**	2	2	resinous, vitreous	transparent, translucent	yellow	O
Sulphides and sulphosalts	Arsenopyrite		iron, **arsenic**	6	6	metallic	opaque	white, grey	M
	Boulangerite		**lead**	6.2	3	metallic	opaque	grey, black	M
	Bournonite		**lead**, copper	5.9	3	metallic	opaque	grey, black	O
	Chalcopyrite		**copper**, iron	4.3	4	metallic	opaque	yellow	TE
	Cinnabar		**mercury**	8.1	2.5	adamantine	translucent	red	R
	Cobaltite		**cobalt**, arsenic	6.3	5.5	metallic	opaque	white	C
	Enargite		**copper**, arsenic	4.5	3	metallic	opaque	grey, black	O
	Galena		**lead**	7.6	3	metallic	opaque	grey	C
	Marcasite		iron	4.8	6.5	metallic	opaque	yellow	O
	Molybdenite		**molybdenum**	4.7	1.5	metallic	opaque	grey	H
	Orpiment		**arsenic**	3.5	2	resinous	translucent	yellow	M
	Pyrite		iron	5	6.5	metallic	opaque	yellow	C
	Pyrrhotite		iron	4.7	4.5	metallic	opaque	yellow	H
	Rammelsbergite		**nickel**, arsenic	7	6	metallic	opaque	white	O
	Realgar		**arsenic**	3.5	2	resinous	translucent	red, orange	M
	Sphalerite		**zinc**	4	4	metallic	translucent, opaque	brown	M
	Stibnite		**antimony**	4.6	2	metallic	opaque	grey	C
	Tennantite		**copper**, iron	5.1	4.5	metallic	opaque	grey	O
	Tetrahedrite		**copper**, iron	5.1	4.5	metallic	opaque	grey, black	C
Halides	Atacamite		copper, chlorine	3.8	3.5	vitreous, greasy	transparent	green	O
	Boleite		lead, copper					blue	O
	Fluorite		**fluorine**	3.2	4	vitreous	transparent, translucent	white, black, blue, red, green, etc.	C
	Rock salt		**salt**	2.2	2	greasy, vitreous	transparent, translucent	colorless, white reddish	C
Hydroxides	Brookite		titanium	4.1	6	vitreous	translucent, opaque	brown, black	O
	Corundum	ruby / sapphire	aluminium	4	9	adamantine, vitreous	transparent, opaque	red, blue, yellow, etc.	R
	Cuprite		**copper**	6.1	4	adamantine	translucent, opaque	red	C
	Goethite		iron	4.3	5	adamantine	opaque	brown	O
	Haematite		**iron**	5.2	6	metallic	opaque	grey, black	R
	Magnetite		**iron**	5.2	5.5	metallic	opaque	black	C
	Manganite		**manganese**	4.3	4	metallic	opaque	grey, black	M
	Opal		silicon	2.3	6.5	vitreous	transparent, translucent	various, iridescent	/

Oxides &

Mineral	Variety	Composition	Hardness	Density	Luster	Transparency	Color	R
Quartz	amethyst, rock crystal, citrine, cairngorm, smoky, chalcedony (carnelian, sardonyx, chrysoprase, lussatite, agate), jasper	silicon	7	2.6	vitreous	transparent, translucent	colorless, various	R
Rutile		**titanium**	6.5	4.2	adamantine	opaque	brown, red	TE
Tantalite		iron, manganese **tantalum, niobium**	6.5	8	metallic	opaque	black	O

Carbonates (nitrates & borates)

Mineral	Variety	Composition	Hardness	Density	Luster	Transparency	Color	R
Aragonite		calcium	4	3	vitreous, greasy	transparent, translucent	colorless, brown	O
Aurichalcite		zinc, copper	1.5	4.2	silky, pearly	translucent	blue, green	O
Azurite		copper	4	3.8	vitreous	transparent, opaque	blue	M
Calcite	Iceland spar	calcium	3	2.7	vitreous, pearly	transparent, opaque	colorless, various	R
Cerussite		**lead**	3	6.5	adamantine	transparent, opaque	colorless, white, black, yellow	O
Dolomite		calcium, **magnesium**	4	2.9	vitreous, dull	translucent, opaque	colorless, yellow, brown, pink	R
Hydrozincite		**zinc**	2.5	3.8	dull	opaque	white, yellowish	M
Malachite		copper	4	4	silky, vitreous	translucent, opaque	green	M
Phosgenite		lead	2.5	6.1	adamantine, waxy	transparent, translucent	white, yellow, brown	TE
Rhodochrosite		**manganese**	4.5	3.7	vitreous	translucent	pink, red	R
Siderite		iron	4	4	vitreous, pearly	translucent, opaque	colorless, yellow, brown	R
Smithsonite		zinc	5	4.4	vitreous, greasy	translucent, opaque	colorless, yellow, green, blue	R

Sulphates (chromates, molybdates & tungstates)

Mineral	Variety	Composition	Hardness	Density	Luster	Transparency	Color	R
Anglesite		**lead**	4.3	6	adamantine	transparent, translucent	white, grey, black	O
Anhydrite		calcium	3.5	3	vitreous, greasy	transparent, translucent	white, blue, red	O
Barite		**barium**	3.5	4.5	vitreous, pearly	transparent, opaque	colorless, yellow, grey	O
Celestite		**strontium**	3.5	4	vitreous, pearly	transparent, opaque	colorless, blue, red	O
Crocoite		lead	3	6	adamantine	translucent	yellow, orange	M
Gypsum	desert rose	calcium	2	2.3	vitreous, pearly	transparent, opaque	colorless, white, brown, yellow	M
Linarite		lead, copper	2.5	5.3	vitreous	translucent	blue	M
Scheelite		calcium, **tungsten**	5	6.1	greasy	transparent, translucent	white, yellow, brown	TE
Wolframite	huebnerite	iron, manganese, **tungsten**	4.5	7.5	metallic	translucent	brown	M
Wulfenite		lead, molybdenum	2.5	6.9	resinous, adamantine	translucent	yellow, brown, red	TE

Phosphates (arsenates & vanadates)

Mineral	Variety	Composition	Hardness	Density	Luster	Transparency	Color	R
Adamite		zinc	3.5	4.4	vitreous	transparent, translucent	yellow, green, pink	O
Apatite	moroxite	calcium, **phosphorous**	5	3.2	vitreous, greasy	translucent, transparent	colorless, white, green, blue	H
Autunite		**uranium**, calcium	2.5	3.1	vitreous, pearly	translucent	yellow, green	TE
Brazilianite		sodium, aluminum	5.5	3	vitreous	transparent	yellow	M
Duftite						translucent	green	O
Erythrite		cobalt	2	3	adamantine, earthy	transparent, translucent	pink	M
Lazulite		iron, magnesium	5.5	3.1	vitreous	translucent	blue	M
Libethenite		copper	4	3.8	resinous	translucent	green	O
Mimetite		lead	4	7.3	adamantine, greasy	translucent	yellow, brown	H
Minyulite		potassium, aluminum						
Purpurite		manganese, iron	3.4	4.5	metallic, pearly	opaque	red, violet	O
Pyromorphite	campylite	**lead**		7.3	adamantine, greasy	translucent	yellow, brown, green	H
Roselite		calcium, cobalt	4	4	vitreous		pink	M

CLASS	MINERAL	VARIETY	PRINCIPAL ELEMENTS	DENSITY	HARDNESS	LUSTRE	TRANSPARENCY	COLOR	CRYSTAL SYSTEM
Phosphates (arsenates & vanadates)	Turquoise		copper, aluminum	2.8	6	vitreous, waxy	translucent	blue	TR
	Vanadinite	endlichite	lead, **vanadium**	7	3	resinous	translucent	red, orange, brown	H
	Vivianite		iron	2.7	1.5	vitreous	transparent, opaque	green, blue	M
	Wavellite		aluminium	2.4	4	vitreous, pearly	translucent	white, green	O
Silicates — Independent Tetrahedral	Andalusite		aluminum	3.2	7.5	vitreous, greasy	translucent, opaque	red, yellow, white	O
	Disthene		aluminum	3.5	5	vitreous, pearly	translucent, transparent	colorless, blue, red	TR
	Garnet	pyrope, almandite, spessartite, grossularite, andradite (demantoid), uvarovite	magnesium, iron manganese	4.3	7.5	vitreous, resinous	transparent, opaque	red, brown, yellow, green	C
	Olivine		magnesium, iron	3.3	7	vitreous	transparent, translucent	green	O
	Staurolite		aluminum, iron	3.7	7.5	vitreous, greasy	translucent, opaque	brown	O
	Topaz		aluminum	3.6	8	vitreous	transparent, translucent	colorless, yellow, blue, green	O
	Zircon	jargon, hyacinth	**zirconium**	4.7	7.5	adamantine, greasy	transparent, opaque	colorless, yellow, red	TE
Double Tetrahedral	Epidote		calcium, iron	3.4	7	vitreous	translucent, opaque	green	M
	Hemimorphite		**zinc**	3.4	5	vitreous	transparent, translucent	white, green, blue	O
	Idocrase		calcium, iron, magnesium	3.4	6.5	vitreous, greasy	transparent, translucent	yellow, green, brown	TE
	Zoisite	tanzanite	calcium, aluminum	3.4	6	vitreous, pearly	translucent	grey, blue, pink	O
Ring	Axinite		calcium, iron, manganese	3.3	7	vitreous	transparent, translucent	violet, pink, yellow	TR
	Benitoite		barium, titanium	3.7	6.5	vitreous	transparent, translucent	blue	H
	Beryl	emerald, aquamarine, morganite, heliodor	aluminium, beryllium	2.7	8	vitreous	transparent, translucent	green, blue, yellow, pink	H
	Dioptase		copper	3.3	5	vitreous	transparent, translucent	green	R
	Tourmaline	achroite, dravite, elbaite (rubellite, indicolite), schorl	boron, aluminum, iron, lithium, magnesium	3.2	7.5	vitreous	transparent, opaque	colorless, various	R
Chain	Actinolite		calcium, iron, magnesium	3.2	6	vitreous	transparent, translucent	white, grey, green	M
	Diopside		calcium, magnesium	3.3	5.6	vitreous, greasy	transparent, translucent	green, grey	M
	Neptunite		sodium, potassium	3.2	6	vitreous	translucent	black	M
	Okenite					pearly		white	TR
	Prehnite		calcium, aluminum	2.9	6.5	vitreous	translucent	white, green	O
	Spodumene	hiddenite, kunzite	**lithium**, aluminum	3.2	7	vitreous	transparent, translucent	green, pink, yellow	M

Category		Mineral	Elements	Density	Hardness	Luster	Transparency	Color	Crystal system
Silicates	Sheet	Apophyllite	potassium, calcium	2.4	5	vitreous, pearly	transparent, translucent	white, green, pink	TE
		Chrysocolla	copper	2.4	4	vitreous, greasy	translucent, opaque	green, blue	M
		Kammererite	chromium	3	2.6	pearly, greasy	transparent, translucent	green, violet	TR
		Kaolinite	aluminum	2.6	2.5	dull	opaque	white	M
		Mica { phlogopite, lepidolite, muscovite (fuchsite…), biotite	potassium, aluminum	3	3	vitreous, pearly	transparent, translucent	green, yellow, brown, lilac	M
		Serpentine { asbestos, garnierite	magnesium	2.6	4	greasy, waxy	translucent, opaque	green	M
	Framework	Albite { cleavelandite, aventurine	sodium	2.6	6	vitreous, pearly	translucent, opaque	white, red, grey	TR
		Heulandite	calcium	2.2	4	pearly, vitreous,	transparent, translucent	white, red	M
		Labradorite	sodium, calcium	2.7	6	vitreous, pearly	translucent, opaque	grey (iridescent)	TR
		Lazurite lapis lazuli (rock)	sodium, calcium	2.4	5.5	vitreous, greasy	translucent, opaque	blue	C
		Microcline amazonstone	potassium	2.6	6	vitreous	translucent	white, pink, green	TR
		Natrolite	sodium	2.2	5.5	vitreous	transparent, translucent	white, red	O
		Oligoclase sunstone	sodium	2.6	6	vitreous, pearly	translucent, opaque	blue	TR
		Orthoclase { adularia, moonstone	potassium	2.6	6	vitreous, pearly	translucent, opaque	white, grey, pink	M
		Stilbite	calcium, sodium	2.2	4	vitreous, pearly	transparent, translucent	white, yellow, brown	M
Organic compounds		Amber	fossilized resin	1	2.5	resinous	transparent, translucent	yellow, brown	/

Elements in bold indicate that a mineral is used as an ore for that element. Crystal system (C = cubic; H = hexagonal; M = monoclinic; O = orthorhombic; R = rhombohedral; TE = tetragonal; TR = triclinic)

INDEX

Numbers in bold refer to pages of text; words in italics refer to topics discussed in the book.

The author and the photographer would like to thank the
following for their assistance in the making of this book:

**The Natural History Museum at Autun for the fossils,
The Natural History Museums at Lyon, Lille and Vienna,
M. Henri-Jean Schubel,
M. Richard Eigenheer, at Franconville,
for the semiprecious stones and the landscape minerals,
the jeweler Chaumet, Place Vendôme, Paris,
who generously allowed us to photograph their
finest stones and items of jewelery,
and individual collectors who wished to remain anonymous,
without whose help this book would not have been possible.**